The Soul of the World
∎∎∎∎∎∎∎∎

Roger Scruton

The Soul of the World

■■■■■■■■

PRINCETON UNIVERSITY PRESS

PRINCETON AND OXFORD

Requests for permission to reproduce material from this work
should be sent to Permissions, Princeton University Press

Published by Princeton University Press, 41 William Street,
Princeton, New Jersey 08540

In the United Kingdom: Princeton University Press, 6 Oxford
Street, Woodstock, Oxfordshire OX20 1TW

press.princeton.edu

Excerpt from Philip Larkin's poem "Aubade" reproduced
with permission from Faber and Faber Ltd.

Library of Congress Cataloging-in-Publication Data

Scruton, Roger.
The soul of the world / Roger Scruton.
pages cm
Includes bibliographical references and index.
ISBN 978-0-691-16157-0 (hardcover : alk. paper) 1. Faith. I. Title.
BL626.3.S38 2013
202—dc23
2013027012

British Library Cataloging-in-Publication Data is available

This book has been composed in Sabon Next Pro
and Chaparral Pro

Printed on acid-free paper. ∞

Printed in the United States of America

1 3 5 7 9 10 8 6 4 2

Contents

∎∎∎∎∎∎∎

Preface
■■■■■■■

This book is based on the Stanton Lectures, delivered in the Michaelmas (fall) term of 2011, in the Divinity Faculty of the University of Cambridge. My intention has been to draw on philosophical discussions of mind, art, music, politics, and law in order to define what is at stake in the current disputes over the nature and ground of religious belief. I regard my argument as making room, in some measure, for the religious worldview, while stopping well short of vindicating the doctrine or practice of any particular faith. Here and there I have given references; but for the most part the manner is informal, and allusions to other writers more conversational than scholarly. Chapters 5 and 6 revisit themes from my Gifford Lectures of 2010 given at St Andrews, and published in 2012 as *The Face of God*. However, they present those themes in another context and cast a rather different light on them. In chapter 6, I build on arguments that are spelled out at greater length in *The Aesthetics of Architecture* (1979, reissued 2013), and in *The Classical Vernacular: Architectural Principles in an Age of Nihilism* (1994). In chapter 7 I revisit topics explored more thoroughly in *The Aesthetics of Music* (1997), and *Understanding Music* (2009). Looking back on those four books, from the perspective offered by the Stanton Lectures, I have come to see more clearly that the positions that naturally appeal to me in aesthetics also suggest a theological elaboration.

I am very grateful to the Faculty of Divinity at Cambridge University for inviting me to give these lectures, and to the lively audiences who turned up each week to encourage me. I am particularly grateful to Douglas Hedley for his support and for getting me to think about the questions afresh. Previous versions of this book have been read by Fiona Ellis, Robert Grant, Douglas Hedley, Anthony O'Hear, and David Wiggins, and I am very grateful to them for their helpful comments. I am grateful too for the illuminating comments provided by the two anonymous readers consulted by Princeton University Press, as well as to Ben Tate of Princeton University Press for his encouragement.

Scrutopia, May 2013

The Soul of the World

1

■■■■■■■■

Believing in God

The currently fashionable discussions of religious belief arose partly in response to the confrontation between Christianity and modern science, and partly in response to the attacks of 9/11, which drew attention to another confrontation, between Islam and the modern world. In both confrontations, as popularly understood, reason points one way, and faith the other. And if faith justifies murder, faith is not an option.

However, the two confrontations have entirely different origins. One is intellectual, the other emotional. One concerns the nature of reality; the other concerns how we should live. Public intellectuals who have espoused the atheist cause often give the impression that religion is defined by a comprehensive explanation of the world, one that incidentally brings comfort and hope, but which, like every explanation, can be refuted by the evidence. But the religion of the Islamists is not like that. It is not primarily an attempt to explain the world, or to show the place of creation in the course of nature. It originates in a need for sacrifice and obedience. No doubt Islamists entertain many metaphysical beliefs, including the belief that the world was created by Allah. But they also believe that they are subject to Allah's commands, that they are called to sacrifice themselves on Allah's behalf, and that their lives will acquire a meaning when thrown away for Allah's sake. Those beliefs are more important to them than the metaphysics, and will survive any niggling attempt to refute the basic tenets of theology. They express an emotional need that precedes rational argument and which shapes the conclusions of theology in advance.

This emotional need can be widely observed, and not only among explicitly religious communities. The desire for sacrifice is rooted deep in all of us, and it is called upon not only by religions but also by secular communities, especially in times of emergency and war. Indeed, if Durkheim is to be followed, this is the core religious experience: the experience of myself as a *member* of something, called upon to renounce my interests for the sake of the group and to celebrate my membership of the group in acts of devotion which might have no other justification than that they are commanded.[1] Others have emphasized the connection between sacrifice and meaning. Patočka, for example, argues that the meaning of life, even of life in the godless twentieth century, resides in the thing for which life—one's own life—can be sacrificed. This striking idea had a profound impact on Central European thought in the communist years, and notably on the writings of Václav Havel.[2] For it suggests that, in totalitarian societies, where the capacity for self-sacrifice is worn thin by the relentless stream of petty punishments, nothing stands out as worthy of our care. This is the secular residue of the core religious thought—the thought that the sacred and the sacrificial coincide. Of course, there is the greatest difference in the world between religions that demand self-sacrifice, and those (like that of the Aztecs) that demand the sacrifice of others. If there is anything that could be called progress in the religious history of mankind, it resides in the gradual preference for the self over the other as the primary sacrificial victim. It is precisely in this that the Christian religion rests its moral claim.

Religion and Evolutionary Psychology

We live in an age of debunking explanations, and the once-popular debunkings of the sociologists are now in their turn debunked by evolutionary psychology. There is a widespread sense that social facts that were previously understood as part of "culture" are now to be explained as adaptations, and that, when we have so explained them, we have removed their aura, so to speak, deprived them of any

---

[1] Émile Durkheim, *The Elementary Forms of the Religious Life* (1912), trans. Carol Cosman and Mark Sydney Cladis (Oxford: Oxford University Press, 2001).

[2] Jan Patočka, *Two Studies of Masaryk* and *Heretical Essays in the Philosophy of History*, trans. E. Kohák (Chicago: Open Court, 1996). Václav Havel, "Politics and Conscience," available in several collections of Havel's essays.

independent hold on our beliefs and emotions, and reduced them to aspects of our biology. The Durkheimian account of religion has been pressed in this direction. Religions survive and gain a following, it is said, because they further the reproductive "strategies" of our genes.[3] By belonging to a group whose members are bound by the rule of sacrifice, you obtain substantial reproductive benefits—territory, security, cooperation, and collective defense. Hence religions do not merely encourage and demand sacrifice: they show a consuming interest in the reproductive life of their members. The gods assemble at those rites of passage in which one generation prepares the way for, and concedes victory to, its successor—at birth, coming of age, marriage, and death. They are fascinated by our sexual habits, insisting in certain cases on genital mutilation, circumcision, and complicated rituals of sexual purity. They have set their faces against incest, adultery, and promiscuous sex, and in general constrain our sexual lives along the path that favors future children over present pleasures, and the transfer of social capital over the squandering of moral resources. So closely do traditional religions fit to the strategies of our genes, and so callously do they seem to favor the genotype over the phenotype, that it is tempting to say that there is little or nothing more to be understood by the one who is seeking an explanation of the religious urge. It is an adaptation like any other, and if it seems to be rooted so deeply within us as to be beyond the reach of rational argument, this is entirely to be expected, since that is how adaptations are passed on.

Adopting the point of view of evolutionary psychology, therefore, and taking on board both the recent defenses of "group selection," and the attack on the "standard social science model" of social behavior, we arrive at a picture of religious belief that seems entirely to discount its rational credentials, as both illusory in themselves and irrelevant to the form and the force of religious feeling.[4] It is important to face up to this kind of claim at the outset, since one of my

[3] See David Sloan Wilson, *Darwin's Cathedral: Evolution, Religion, and the Nature of Society* (Chicago: University of Chicago Press, 2002).

[4] On the arguments for group selection, see Edward O. Wilson, *The Social Conquest of Earth* (New York: Liveright, 2012). On the demise of the "standard social science model," see Jerome Berkow, Leda Cosmides, and John Tooby, eds., *The Adapted Mind: Evolutionary Psychology and the Generation of Culture* (New York: Oxford University Press, 1995).

purposes will be to suggest that functional explanations of the evolutionary kind have no bearing on the content of our religious beliefs and emotions.

My reasons for saying this are two. The first is this: explanations of the kind popularized in the contemporary literature overlook the aspect of our mental states that is most important to us, and through which we understand and act upon each other's motives, namely, their intentionality or "aboutness." The thought here is well illustrated by the incest taboo. Freud argued that the taboo is strong because it stands in the path of a strong desire. We are revolted by incest because we unconsciously want to do it. That explanation is rejected by evolutionary psychologists, who tell us that the revulsion against incest comes about not because we want to do it, but because we don't want to do it. We don't want to do it, because our not wanting has been selected for by evolution. Human beings not repelled by incest have for the most part died out.

Scientifically speaking, there is no doubt which theory we should choose. Freud is not giving a true causal explanation of the incest taboo, but rather a redescription of it as part of a rational strategy, though one pursued by the unconscious. In order to make his explanation work, he has to invent an entity, the unconscious, for the existence of which we have no independent evidence, or evidence that comes only from more pseudo-explanations of the same kind. Nevertheless, we might feel a measure of sympathy for Freud. For he wants to explain not only why incest is forbidden, but also why the *thought* of it affects us in the deepest reaches of our being. The disgust we feel, and which led Oedipus to stab out his eyes and Jocasta to hang herself, has a peculiar intentionality or directedness. It focuses on the idea that this is my sister, mother, brother, or father, and it tells me that any sexual contact would be a kind of pollution, a spoiling of something that will never afterward be the same. Incest is therefore seen as an *existential* crime, one that changes what we are, both to ourselves and to others.

From the point of view of evolution it would be sufficient that incest should arouse disgust, in the way that rotten flesh or feces arouse disgust. The thought processes add nothing to the reproductive function. On the contrary, they compromise it, by winding it into the peculiar intentionality of our personal relations, causing us to lift this reproductive error out of the dark realm of biology into the light of moral reflection, and so to find not only reasons against incest, but reasons *for* it too—of the kind familiar to the Egyptian pharaohs, or the kind that impressed themselves on Siegmund and Sieglinde in their sole moment of joy.

But this means that there is something in the incest taboo that the evolutionary explanation does not account for: namely, its "about-ness," the aspect of it that is most important to us, and through which incest enters into our thinking and is in turn transformed by that thinking into something that may be wanted as well as forbidden. And that, surely, is what appeals to us in Freud—namely, that his explanation, however weak as science, is an attempt to account for the specificity of the incest taboo, and to show why we, rational, personal, self-conscious beings, experience it as a *taboo*, while other animals simply don't do it (unless, of course, they do).

Internal and External Viewpoints

This leads me to my second reason for disregarding evolutionary explanations, which is that they cannot take note of the internal order of our states of mind. Evolution explains the connection between our thoughts and the world, and between our desires and their fulfillment, in pragmatic terms. We think and feel in ways that promote the goal of reproduction. But our mental states have no such goal. We pursue the true, the good, and the beautiful, even though the false, the nasty, and the messy might have been just as useful to our genes. The case of mathematics is especially vivid. We could have evolved without the capacity to understand the realm of mathematical truth and still be just as well adapted to solve the small-scale arithmetical conundrums of the hunter-gatherer. So what is it that explains the crucial fact: that our thinking "latches on" to a realm of necessary truth, reaching infi-nitely beyond the puzzles that we need to solve? Once over the hump, from an innumerate to a numerate creature, the human species was able to run forward into this new pasture, enjoying its wonderful fruit of futile knowledge, building theories and proofs, and in gen-eral transforming its vision of the world without any benefits to its reproductive potential—or with benefits that come far too late to exert any evolutionary pressure in favor of the research that produces them. Evolutionary theory can give us a map of how the basic operations of arithmetic arise, but you could understand that map without understanding mathematics. And out of mathematical reasoning there arises the *true* philosophical question, the question that no amount of biology could ever solve: namely, what is mathematics *about*? What in the world *are* numbers, sets, and transfinite cardinals?

Nor is mathematics a special case. There are many ways in which people gain understanding of the world by interpreting signs and symbols, and even if this confers an evolutionary advantage, interpretation also unfolds another vision of the world than that contained in the theory of evolution.[5] Language is the most striking example of this. We don't know how it arose. But we do know that language enables us to understand the world as no dumb animal could possibly understand it. Language enables us to distinguish truth and falsehood; past, present, and future; possible, actual, and necessary, and so on. It is fair to say that we live in another world from nonlinguistic creatures. They live immersed in nature; we stand forever at its edge. Since emotions and motives are founded on thoughts, our emotional life and our motives to act will be of an entirely different kind from those of the other animals. This is surely why we should question those theories of altruism as an "evolutionally stable strategy"—theories defended and refined by John Maynard Smith, David Sloan Wilson, Elliott Sober, Matt Ridley, and others.[6] For altruism in people is not just an instinctive thing, even if it has an instinctive component. It is also a considered response, based sometimes on *agape* or neighbor love, sometimes on complex interpersonal emotions like pride and shame, which are in turn founded on the recognition of the other as another like me. In all cases altruism in people involves the judgment that what is bad for *the other* is something that *I* have a motive to remedy. And the existence of that thought is precisely what is not explained by the theory that tells us that altruism is also a dominant strategy in the game of reproduction.

[5] For some of the arguments around this issue, see Anthony O'Hear, *Beyond Evolution: Human Nature and the Limits of Evolutionary Explanation* (Oxford: Oxford University Press, 1997). The argument against naturalism is set out more formally in Alvin Plantinga, *Warrant and Proper Function* (Oxford: Oxford University Press, 1993), chap. 12.

[6] See in particular Matt Ridley, *The Origins of Virtue* (New York: Viking, 1996).

Just as mathematics opens before us the world of mathematical necessities, so does morality open the world of values, and science the world of natural laws. We think *about* the world, and this means thinking beyond our genetic needs, to the world of which we are a part. From the evolutionary point of view it is a sheer chance that we made this step, from useful instinct to directed thought. One philosopher, Thomas Nagel, has argued that such a thing cannot be a mere chance, suggesting that the universe must therefore be governed by teleological laws. On Nagel's view it is a *law of nature* that our scientific thinking tends toward the truth, our morality toward the good, and maybe (though he doesn't go this far) our tastes toward the beautiful.[7] I return to that radical response in later chapters. Whatever we think of it, we must acknowledge that evolutionary psychology cannot give a complete picture either of our states of mind, or of the universe that is represented in them. The theory of evolution is itself a scientific theory. We have reason to believe it only because we trust that the directedness of our thinking is not an accidental by-product of the evolutionary process but an independent guide to the way things are, whose credentials go beyond its adaptive benefits. The theory of evolution may seem to offer an outside view of science. But it is written in the language of science. If the theory really did offer an outside view, then it could conceivably have led to the conclusion that false beliefs have a better survival value than true ones, and therefore that all our beliefs are likely to be false. But what then of the theory that tells us so? If true, it is likely to be false. In other words, if we attempt to reach the high ground of naturalism by this route, we encounter a version of the liar paradox: an obstacle to which there is only one response—turn back!

Naturalism

This brings me back to religion. To explain religion in terms of its reproductive function is to leave unexplained and indeed unperceived the central core of the phenomenon, which is the religious *thought*— the *aboutness* of the urge to sacrifice, of the need to worship and obey,

[7]Thomas Nagel, *Mind and Cosmos* (New York: Oxford University Press, 2012).

of the trepidation of the one who approaches holy and forbidden things and who prays for their permission.

Of course, it does not follow that the explanation of this thought is to be found elsewhere than in the biological and social circumstances of the person in whom it occurs. Religious thoughts might be like dream thoughts, which we trace not to the objects represented in them, but to things going on in the nervous system during sleep. Indeed, there are cultures in which dreams are regarded as the principal vehicle through which the gods and their doings make themselves known. For that very reason, however, they do not share our theories concerning the bodily origin of dreams. Rather, they think of dreams as giving access to another realm and to the beings that haunt it.

It is easy to see, from the comparison with dreams, that there is a real problem about the *epistemology* of religious thoughts. The theological tradition to which we are heirs—which begins with Plato and Aristotle, and which achieves its high point of sophistication in medieval times, with Avicenna, Averroës, Maimonides, and Aquinas—tends to the view that there is one and only one God, who is the creator and sustainer of the physical world, but who is also transcendental, outside space and time, and therefore not *part* of the physical world. Fast-forwarding to Kant's *Critique of Pure Reason*, and then a bit further to Einstein's theory of relativity, we move to the conclusion that such a God cannot be part of the system of causes, since the space-time continuum is the matrix in which causes occur. If there is such a thing as (in Eliot's words) "the point of intersection of the timeless with time," it is not discoverable to physics. In which case there can be no causal connection between God and our thoughts of him.

Quine and others have argued that epistemology should be "naturalized," so as to provide the empirical explanation of our knowledge, rather than some putative a priori ground for it.[8] According to those thinkers we should look on epistemological questions from outside, as questions concerning the relation between an organism and its environment. True beliefs and veridical perceptions are beliefs and perceptions that link the organism to its environment in the right way, so as to give reliable information about their causes. Illusions and

---

[8] W. V. Quine, "Ontological Relativity," *Journal of Philosophy* (1968), reprinted in *Ontological Relativity and Other Essays* (New York: Columbia University Press, 1969).

false beliefs exemplify "deviant causal chains," and are to be explained in some other way than by reference to the objects represented in them—as dreams, for example, are explained. Our ontology, on this view, consists of all those items that are referred to in the true explanation of our beliefs. It does not contain the creatures of our dreams or the characters in fiction; nor does it contain the gods and spirits that haunt our lives, however dear to us these are, and however impossible it may be to free ourselves from the belief in their existence.

However, if God is a transcendental being, who lies outside the space-time continuum, then it is a deep, perhaps even a necessary, truth that God has no causal role to play in the beliefs that target him—or in any other event in space and time. If this is sufficient to exclude God from our ontology, then many other things too must be excluded. We also have beliefs about numbers, sets, and other mathematical objects. And these too are outside space and time, or at any rate have no causal role in the physical world. Of course, the status of mathematical truth is, for this very reason, controversial. Does mathematics describe some transcendental realm of eternally existing objects? Or does it in some way outline the laws of thought, but without real ontological commitments? This is not the place to examine those questions, which have absorbed the energies of all the greatest philosophical minds from Plato to the present day. Suffice it to say that there have been advances in sophistication, but no advances in consensus, concerning the issue of mathematical truth. And this means that the issue of theological truth cannot be closed so simply as the atheists wish. Monotheists are constrained by their own theology to accept that the causal explanation of their belief in God can make no reference to the God in whom they believe. That this belief must be explained in terms of biological, social, or cultural processes is a truth contained in the belief itself. So how can those explanations show the belief to be false?

The Real Presence

That is not an argument for the truth of religious belief, but only a suggestion that will shift the onus away from the believer. It is tantamount to the demand that the atheist find arguments directed at the *content* of the belief, rather than arguments directed at its origins. But a new problem now arises, and it is one that has been familiar to Jewish, Christian, and Muslim theology from the early Middle Ages, and this is the problem of God's presence. This problem will be my starting point, and so I need to set it out carefully now.

That God is present among us and communicating directly with us is a central claim of the Old Testament. This "real presence" or *shekhinah* is, however, a mystery. God reveals himself by concealing himself, as he concealed himself from Moses in the burning bush, and as he conceals himself from his worshippers in the Tabernacle (*mishkhan*) and the Holy of Holies. The nouns *shekhinah* and *mishkhan* are both from the verb *shakhan*, to dwell or settle: *sakana* in Arabic, from which is derived the noun *sakīnah*, used here and there in the Koran (e.g., al-Baqara, 2, 248) to describe the peace or comfort that comes from God. Dwelling and settling are the underlying themes of the Torah, which tells the story of the Promised Land, and of the people who finally settle there, to build in Jerusalem the Temple whose design and rituals were given to Moses, and which will be a dwelling place for God. As the narrative makes clear, it is not the chosen people only who are in search of a place to settle: it is God too, who can dwell among them only by being ritually concealed from them. As God says to Moses, no man shall look on my face and live. And the whole tormented story of the relation between God and the chosen people brings home to us the terrible truth, which is that God *cannot* show himself in this world, except by hiding from those whom he traps into trusting him, as he trapped the Jews. The knowledge of his presence comes with the failure to find him.

Metaphysically speaking, this is what we must expect. It is not just that the intervention of a transcendent God in the world of space and time would be a miracle—though miracles, for reasons made clear by Spinoza and Hume, are not the simple exceptions that their defenders make them out to be. It is rather that it is difficult to make sense of the idea that this, here, now is a revelation of an eternal and transcendental being. A direct personal encounter with God, when God is understood in the philosophical way of Avicenna or Aquinas, is no more possible than a direct personal encounter with the number 2. Now you see through a glass darkly, wrote Saint Paul, but then face-to-face.

However, by "then" he meant "beyond the here and now," in the transcendental realm where God resides. Saint Paul may seem to be denying the hidden nature of God; in fact he is affirming it.

And yet the experience of the "real presence" is at the heart of revealed religion, and foundational to the liturgy and ritual both of the synagogue and of the main Christian churches. It is important to grasp this point. Many of those who currently write against religion (and specifically against the Christian religion) seem to think that faith is simply a matter of entertaining beliefs of a cosmological kind, concerning the creation of the world and the hope of eternal life. And these beliefs are imagined to be in some ways rivals to the theories of physics, and exposed to refutation by all that we know of the evolution of the universe. But the real *phenomena* of faith are nothing like that. They include prayer and the life of prayer; the love of God and the sense of his presence in the life of the faithful; obedience and submission in the face of temptation and the things of this world; the experience of certain times, places, objects, and words as "sacred," which is to say, in Durkheim's phrase, as "set aside and forbidden," reserved for uses that can be understood only on the assumption that these experiences mediate between this world and another that is not otherwise revealed to us.

Two immensely difficult questions arise from those thoughts. They are not questions that trouble ordinary believers. But they are fundamental to understanding what is at stake in the religious worldview. The first is metaphysical, namely, how is it possible for the transcendental to manifest itself in the empirical—for the eternal God to be a real presence in the life of his earthly worshippers? The second is conceptual, namely, what is the *thought* that animates the encounter with sacred things: what concepts, beliefs, and perceptions define the intentionality of faith? The first of those questions is one that I shall postpone, since I don't believe it can be answered until we have become clear about the second question. We rightly think that there is something mysterious and perhaps inexplicable about the "real presence." But nobody who has the experience of that thing is likely to think it to be simply an illusion: it comes to us with a self-verifying character that silences skepticism, even if it also calls out for interpretation. Such was the *nuit de feu* of Pascal: the night of 23 November

1654 when, for two hours, he experienced the total certainty that he was in the presence of God—"the God of Abraham, of Isaac and of Jacob, not the God of the philosophers and the wise men," in other words a personal God, intimately revealed, not conjured by abstract argument. *Père juste, le monde ne t'a point connu, mais moi, je t'ai connu,* he wrote then, on the scrap of paper on which he recorded the experience: astonishing words, which only total conviction could have engendered.

Religion and Magic

When anthropologists first addressed the issue of the religious frame of mind, they very quickly discovered patterns of thinking that were both widespread among human beings, and also difficult or impossible to assimilate to the aims and methods of scientific inquiry. Although Sir James Frazer writes (in *The Golden Bough*) as though magical ways of thinking begin life as an attempt at science—being used in order to predict and control the reach of human actions—it is surely very clear both that magic does not, as science does, represent the world as something wholly independent of the will of the one who is seeking to understand it, and also that magic aims less to predict results than to command them. The primary device of magic is the spell. Unlike a scientific inference, a spell is addressed directly to the natural world, commanding it to obey the wishes of the one who casts it. Even if the magician needs to summon occult powers, to enlist the cooperation of gods and spirits, he is not trying to discover how nature works, or to use the laws of nature in order to produce some desired effect. He is trying to bypass prediction entirely, so as to address nature as a subject like himself—as something that can submit to his commands and be moved by his beseeching.[9]

[9]The argument that magic is *transcended* by religion, since the first acts directly on nature while the second invokes a supernatural being who acts on our behalf, was, in the wake of Frazer, widely accepted—see, for example, W. Warde Fowler's Gifford Lectures, *The Religious Experience of the Roman People* (London: Macmillan, 1911). I doubt that the distinction has much weight in the thinking of anthropologists today.

That attempt would be condemned by many people as superstition and idolatry. But, even if we put magical thinking behind us, there remains in the religious frame of mind the core thought of another subject, the god toward whom one's thoughts and feelings are directed. The real presence is not that of a mysterious nonentity, a flitting ghost, or a vision. It is the presence of a subject, a first-person singular who can be addressed, implored, reasoned with, and loved. Religious people may not entirely and completely believe that they are addressing another subject in their prayers—for their faith may be weak and vacillating, or they may enter the sacred moment with a measure of aesthetic distance, or in one way or another they may fail entirely to give themselves up to the immediate experience. Nevertheless their state of mind is "subject directed." It has the particular intentionality that informs all our interpersonal attitudes, and which adheres to them because they are forms of *address* from one person to another: a readiness to give and accept reasons, to make demands, and also to respond to demands, a recognition of mutual freedom and all the benefits and dangers that are implied by it. A readiness, as we might put it, remembering the Old Testament story of Jacob and the angel, to "wrestle with God"—the idea contained in the name *Isra-el*.

People who are looking for God are not looking for the proof of God's existence; nor would it help them to be persuaded, say, by Aquinas's Five Ways, or by Avicenna's version of the cosmological argument, or by any of those specious arguments that have been doing the rounds in recent years, concerning the improbability that the universe should be just as it is, and there be no God as its creator.[10] They are not looking for arguments but for a subject-to-subject encounter, which occurs in this life, but which also in some way reaches beyond this life. Those who claim to have found God always write or speak in those terms, as having found the intimacy of a personal encounter and a moment of trust. The great witnesses to this—Saint Teresa of Avila, Margery Kempe, Saint John of the Cross, Rumi, Pascal—surely

[10]See, for example, Richard Swinburne, "Argument from the Fine-Tuning of the Universe," in *Physical Cosmology and Philosophy*, ed. John A. Leslie (New York: Macmillan, 1990), pp. 160–87. This and similar proposals are criticized by Elliott Sober, in "The Design Argument," in *The Blackwell Companion to Philosophy of Religion*, ed. W. Mann (Oxford: Blackwell, 2004), pp. 117–47.

persuade us that one part, at least, of the encounter with God lies in the irruption into consciousness of an intersubjective state of mind, but one that connects with no merely human subject. And included within that state of mind is the sense of reciprocity: the sense of being targeted by the Other, I to I.

But that is not the end of the story. It has been evident at least since Durkheim that religion is a *social* phenomenon, and the individual search for God answers to a deep need of the species. Human beings desire to "throw in their lot" with something, to cease to be cast out, rejected, *geworfen*, mere individuals, and to belong, even if the price of doing so is submission or *islām*. People join together in many different ways, and some, like hermits, seek to be alone with their God. But the normal tendency of the religious urge is toward membership, by which I mean a network of relations that are neither contractual nor negotiated, but which are received as a destiny and a gift. It is one of the weaknesses of modern political philosophy that it makes so little room for relations of this kind—the relations of belonging that precede political choice and make it possible. But, as I argue in chapter 4, they are the core of all true communities, and are recognized precisely by their "transcendent" character—that is to say, their character as arising from outside the arena of individual choice. Durkheim pointed out that you don't merely *believe* a religion but (more importantly) you *belong* to it, and that disputes over religious doctrine are, as a rule, not simply arguments about abstruse questions of metaphysics but attempts to give a viable test of membership, and hence a way of identifying and excluding the heretics who threaten the community from within.

Religion and the Sacred

But what distinguishes religious membership from, say, kinship, nationhood, tribal loyalties, and the sense of territory and customs as "ours"? Durkheim writes that "a religion is a unified system of beliefs and practices relative to sacred things, that is to say, things set apart and forbidden—beliefs and practices which unite into a single moral community, called a 'church,' all those who adhere to them." But his definition simply shifts the problem onto the concepts invoked in it, the concepts of the sacred and the church.

Durkheim's parenthetical characterization of the sacred as "set apart and forbidden" is suggestive, but far from satisfying. We want to know in what way sacred things are set apart, and how forbidden. They are not forbidden in the way that chocolate is forbidden by parents, or drunk driving forbidden by the state. In the religious context that which is forbidden to one person is permitted to or even demanded of another. The host that it is sacrilegious for the ordinary believer to touch can nevertheless be offered to him at the altar from the hands of a priest. And in the Catholic tradition the believer is obliged to take the sacrament twice a year.

One thing is clear, which is that the old theories of magic, associated with Sir Edward Burnett Tylor, Frazer, and the nineteenth-century schools of anthropology, do not explain the sacred. There is a prosaic quality about magic, a here-and-now character, and a practicality too, which have little or nothing in common with the awe-inspiring otherworldliness of sacred things. Consider the examples familiar to us: the Eucharist, and the instruments associated with it; the prayers with which we address God; the Cross, the scroll of the Torah, the pages of the Koran. The faithful approach these things with awe, not because of their magic power, but because they seem to be both *in* our world, and also out of it—a passage between the immediate and the transcendental. They are both present and absent, like the *mishkhan* and what it hides from us.

That indeed seems to be a feature of the sacred in all religions. Sacred objects, words, animals, ceremonies, places, all seem to stand at the horizon of our world, looking out to that which is not of this world, because it belongs in the sphere of the divine, and looking also *into* our world, so as to meet us face-to-face. Through sacred things we can influence and be influenced by the transcendental. If there is to be a real presence of the divine in this world, it must be in the form of some sacred event, moment, place, or encounter: so at least we humans have believed.

There is truth in Durkheim's view that sacred things are in some way forbidden. But what is forbidden is to treat a sacred thing as though it belonged in the ordinary frame of nature: as though it had no mediating role. Treating a sacred thing in this day-to-day way is a *profanation*.[11] One stage beyond profanation is *desecration*, in which a sacred object is deliberately wrenched from its apartness and trampled on or in some way reduced to its opposite, so as to become mean and disgusting. The Judaic tradition is rich in examples of the sacred: the Temple was, indeed, a kind of repository of sacred things, and stood as a symbol of God's protecting presence throughout the great years of Jewish triumph, and also later, when the Jews were able to negotiate sufficient autonomy to retain the Holy City as their own. The destruction of the Temple by the Romans in AD 70 was accompanied by acts of desecration, including the carrying away by pagan hands of the sacred vessels, and the burning of sacred texts. These acts were experienced by the Jews as a profound existential trauma—a repeat of the trauma of the first desecration, some six hundred years earlier, which forms the subject of the Lamentations of Jeremiah. The question in the minds of the Jews at both events was this: these sacred objects are under the special protection of God himself—they *belong* to him, and are *his own*. That is the origin of their sanctity. So if he permits their desecration, this is because he has abandoned us—rejected our gifts to him, and the practices through which we rehearse his presence among us. This is the terrifying thought in the Lamentations, a text that tries to come to terms with the desecration of the Temple by seeing it precisely as God's way of bringing home the fact that he has departed from us, leaving his temple and his people unprotected.

Frazer and his contemporaries were highly impressed by the Polynesian concept of *taboo*, a word that has since entered every language. Objects, people, words, places are taboo when they must be avoided, when they cannot be touched, approached, or perhaps even thought of without contagion. A taboo can be *placed* on something, like a curse; and it can attach itself to any kind of thing—object, animal, food, person, words, places, times. The idea goes hand in hand with the complementary notion of *mana*, which is the spiritual strength

---

[11] See the discussion of the sacred/profane distinction in Mircea Eliade's survey of the anthropological data, *The Sacred and the Profane: The Nature of Religion* (New York: Harcourt, Brace, 1959).

residing in things and radiating from them, by virtue of which they can effect changes in the human environment. There is a whole worldview contained in the ideas of *taboo* and *mana*, and it is not surprising that the early anthropologists tried to generalize those ideas to cover all religions. Thus the dietary laws laid down in Leviticus are often given as an example of taboo.[12] And maybe it is in terms of this concept that we should seek to understand the sacred: a thing becomes sacred when ordinary ways of using it are taboo, and when, in a certain special use, it possesses a *mana* of its own. Is that an advance?

A taboo, Freud believed, exists in order to forbid something that is intensely desired. It is the collective response to individual temptation. The principal arena of temptation is sex, and the principal taboo is that forbidding incest, in particular incest between son and mother—the taboo issued by the primeval father to his sons. In *Totem and Taboo*, therefore, Freud gives a theory of primitive religion on the same lines as the theory of the Oedipus complex. And the theory has an interesting corollary, which is that religious awe and the sense of the sacred belong in the same psychic area as sexual desire and its associated ethic of purity and pollution. Freud arrives at this conclusion by way of the contentious, and indeed discredited, theory of the Oedipus complex. But it is a connection that has been made in different ways down the centuries—for example, in Dante's account of Beatrice, forbidden object of his erotic longing, who reveals to him the mysteries of Paradise.

Many people today would say that Freud's account of taboo is fanciful, a product of the same collection of obsessive themes and hostilities that produced his frankly unbelievable account of infantile sexuality. But there is an interesting thought behind the theory, which is this: the forbidden quality of sacred things is such a strange feature, and puts such intense social and psychological demands on those who receive it, that it must have a special explanation. There must be a way in which this strange idea *enters* into a human community,

---

[12]Though a heroic attempt to justify them in other and more spiritual terms is made by Leon Kass, in his brilliant book *The Hungry Soul: Eating and the Perfection of Our Nature* (Chicago: University of Chicago Press, 1999).

changing it from a loose assemblage of people in competition with each other, into a social unit bound together by its sense of the transcendental significance of the rituals that its members share. *Totem and Taboo* is therefore a theory of "hominization," of the transition from the simian tribe to the human community. According to the theory, this transition is effected by the original sin of parricide, as a result of which the entire community becomes bound by prohibitions and subdued by the unconscious burden of collective guilt. Just such a conception lies behind the equally imaginative theory of the sacred developed by René Girard in *La Violence et le sacré* (1972) and subsequent works. This theory is worth rehearsing now, since my argument will touch on many of the matters that motivate it.

Thoughts on Girard

Girard begins from an observation that no impartial reader of the Hebrew Bible or the Koran can fail to make, which is that monotheistic religion may promise peace, but is also deeply implicated in violence. The God presented in those writings is frequently angry, given to insane fits of destruction and seldom deserving of the epithets bestowed upon him in the Koran—*al-raḥmān al-raḥīm*, "the compassionate, the merciful." He makes outrageous and bloodthirsty demands—such as the demand that Abraham sacrifice his son. This particular demand, pivotal for all three Abrahamic religions, is singled out by Kierkegaard as the ultimate test of faith, to which Abraham must respond by an "infinite resignation," thereby conceding that everything, his son included, belongs to God. Others, by contrast, have seen this story as a provocation, an invitation to condemn religion, as a force that can override even the most binding moral imperatives.[13]

For Girard, however, the story has another significance entirely. It illustrates the true role of religion, not as the cause of violence, but as the solution to it, even if the solution must take the form, as here, of a

---

[13] Kierkegaard's study is *Fear and Trembling* (1843). For the use of the story against the religion conveyed by it, see Paul Cliteur, *The Secular Outlook: In Defence of Moral and Political Secularism* (Oxford: Wiley-Blackwell, 2010).

sacrificial offering. The violence itself comes from another source, and there is no society without it since it is engendered by the very attempt of human beings to live together as individuals, rather than as members of a pack or herd. The same can be said too of the obsession with sexuality: religion is not the cause of this, but an attempt to resolve it. In both those thoughts Girard is close to Freud, and indeed *Totem and Taboo* is one of the most frequently cited works in his discussion.

Girard sees the primeval condition of society as one of conflict. It is in the effort to resolve this conflict that the experience of the sacred is born. This experience comes to us in many forms—in religious ritual, in prayer, in tragedy—but its true origin is in an act of communal violence. Primitive societies emerge from the state of nature and the bondage of animal life, only to be invaded by "mimetic desire," as rivals struggle to match each other's social and material acquisitions, so heightening antagonism and precipitating the cycle of revenge. This human form of violence is not a "war of all against all," of the kind attributed to the state of nature by Hobbes. It is already a social phenomenon, involving a strong sense of the other as another like me. The solution to this kind of violence is to identify a victim, one marked by fate as "outside" the community and therefore not entitled to vengeance against it, who can be the target of the accumulated bloodlust, and who can bring the chain of retribution to an end. Scapegoating is society's way of re-creating "difference" and so restoring itself. By uniting against the scapegoat, people are released from their rivalries and reconciled. Through his death the victim purges society of its violence. His resulting sanctity is the long-term echo of the awe, relief, and visceral reattachment to the community that was experienced at his death. Through incest, kingship, or worldly hubris the victim marks himself out as the outsider, the one who is not with us, and whom we can therefore sacrifice without renewing the cycle of revenge. The victim is thus both sacrificed and sacred, the source of the city's plagues and their cure.

The experience of the sacred is not, on this view, an irrational residue of primitive fears, nor is it a form of superstition that will one day be chased away by science. According to Girard, it is a *solution* to the accumulated aggression that lies in the heart of human communities. However, it is a solution that, in its original version, places violence in the heart of things. In a singular argument, Girard suggests that Jesus was the first scapegoat to understand the need for his own death and to forgive those who inflicted it. And in submitting to this, Girard argues, Jesus gave the best evidence, and perhaps the only possible evidence, of his divine nature. He was the Lamb of God, the innocent victim, and also Emmanuel, God among us, who came to release us from the violence that had hitherto been locked into the heart of our communities.[14] On him all the sins of the world—sins of envy, rivalry, and malice—could be discharged, and he would accept the death that these states of mind are inwardly longing for. This mystical idea is celebrated in the Christian Eucharist, when the communicants rehearse the sacrifice of a God who took their sins upon himself, and so purchased their forgiveness.

Girard's vision of the Eucharist is anticipated in Wagner's *Parsifal*, as is the ineffable peace that flows from the moment of our redemption. The self-sacrifice of the Redeemer turns conflict to forgiveness and violence to peace. Such is the meaning of the sublimely tranquil Good Friday music of act 3, music that conveys the smiling face of the world on the day when the sacrifice is made. Girard's theory of the sacrament is also anticipated by Hegel, who writes that "in the *sacraments* reconciliation is brought into feeling, into the here and now of present and sensible consciousness; and all the manifold actions are embraced under the aspect of *sacrifice*."[15] Girard, like Hegel, takes himself to be describing deep features of the human condition, which can be observed as well in the mystery cults of antiquity and the local shrines of Hinduism as in the everyday rite of the Eucharist. And like Hegel, he wishes to single out the Christian religion for special treatment. The Christian sacraments rehearse the solution that previous explorations of the sacred could not find, which is the self-sacrifice of God.

Whatever its merits as a Christian apologetic, Girard's narrative fails to explain what it is to regard a thing as sacred. Girard draws on the fact that the sacrificial animal is regarded as sacred by those who slaughter it. But why? Does the theory answer that question or does

---

[14] See especially the argument in *Le Bouc émissaire* (Paris: Grasset, 1982).

[15] G.W.F. Hegel, *Lectures on the Philosophy of Religion*, ed. Peter C. Hodgson, trans. Hodgson et al. (Berkeley: University of California Press, 1988), p. 193.

it rather suppose that it is already answered? Retelling the theory in the language of evolutionary psychology avoids that question. You can describe a ritual as an adaptation without mentioning how the participants interpret what they are doing. You might simply suggest that sacrificial rituals overcome aggression between tribal members by providing a substitute target against which rivals can unite. They therefore perpetuate the benefits of group membership. But again there is something missing from the evolutionary explanation, namely, a philosophical account of the *thought* on which our conceptions of the sacred are built. And that thing is missing from Girard's theory too.

Moreover, the theory is not easy to extend to other areas in which we are inclined to speak of sacred things. The ideas of the sacred and the sacramental attach themselves to birth, to sexual union and marriage, and also to the ordinary death of ordinary people—these are all things that are set apart, regarded with awe, in which God is directly concerned, and which can be desecrated. Why are not these just as important as the more explicitly sacrificial aspects of the religious way of life? Rites of passage are surely more basic than ritual sacrifices—sometimes, perhaps, the occasion for ritual sacrifices, but in themselves far more necessary to the psychic health and togetherness of the community than the sacrifice of the occasional scapegoat. The sense of the sacred surely *precedes* ritual sacrifice, is more primitive, more basic, more fundamental to the human condition than any of the phenomena normally invoked to explain it. This does not mean that genealogical accounts of the kind advanced by Girard are of no value. They help to bring out fundamental features of the phenomenon that they purport to explain. But they do not in fact explain it. They have the character—which I shall further analyze in chapter 5—of a "myth of origins," a story that represents the layers of social reality as stages in a temporal process.

Still, we can now say something a little more definite about the intentionality of the religious frame of mind. It is a reaching out from subject to subject; it searches for a relation that is close, intimate, and personal, with a being who is present in this world though not of this world; and in this reaching out there is a movement toward sacrifice, in which both self and other might give themselves completely and thereby achieve a reconciliation that lies beyond the reach of ordinary human dialogue. Maybe this frame of mind is connected to those primitive forms of violence to which Girard alludes. Certainly it resonates with the stories of sacrificial victims, and suggests that there are roots to this state of mind that are far darker than we can, in our daily lives, easily acknowledge. But the essential character of the religious frame of mind is that of an intersubjective awareness in which the readiness for sacrifice is in some way contained. And in judging religions, we are acutely aware of the extent to which the sacrifices they ask for are sacrifices of others or sacrifices of self. It is surely that, above all else, that has entered our awareness through the actions of the Islamist "martyrs."

The Epistemology of the Sacred

The other great question remains, which is the question of veracity. *Is* there anything that answers to this search for the sacred? *Can* the eternal be present among us in the way that rewards our search for it? We must not think of this merely as a theological or metaphysical question. For it is a question that inhabits the religious sentiment itself. It is the source of religious doubt and also the challenge offered to faith. Often, when a faith-community settles on some particular object, or rite, or words as sacred, it *loses* the presence of the thing in question, which retreats into the eternal as did the God of Moses and Abraham when his temple was destroyed. The same retreat into the eternal occurred, at a certain stage, with the God of the Koran. If the Koran is really a revelation from God, spoken by the Eternal, the scholars asked, then how can it exist in time, as a mere text among others, to be interpreted and applied through the arguments of ordinary mortals? This question particularly troubled the 'Asharite school of theology, and the conclusion its scholars drew was that the Koran must be eternal, outside time and change, and therefore not open to interpretation or amendment. From that moment the gate of *ijtihad* (creative interpretation) was closed.[16] To put it from a Christian perspective, the Koran ceased to be a record of God's presence among

---

[16] See Robert Reilly, *The Closing of the Muslim Mind* (Wilmington, DE: ISI Books, 2010).

us, and became the proof of his absence—the trace left behind as he departed forever from our midst. The Sufis did not accept this, and the prayers and invocations of Rumi, Hafiz, and Omar Khayyam call upon God once again as the Friend, who moves among us, who meets us in this world, yet freely and unforeseeably, like the *sakīnah* of the Koran. But as for the Sunni Orthodoxy, which tells us that God revealed himself, but only in a book that exists outside space and time, this leaves the question of God's presence in our world exactly as it was—a question without an answer.

Perhaps something like that is true of the Protestant tradition too. Paul Ricoeur has argued that the task of religion (and he means the Christian religion) in our time is to complete the expulsion of the sacred from the practice of faith—so that we confront God as he is, not confined in this or that moment or this or that corner of the world.[17] Yet we know that this excision of the sacred does not encourage faith but merely deprives it of the soil in which it grows. The real question for religion in our time is not how to excise the sacred, but how to rediscover it, so that the moment of pure intersubjectivity, in which nothing concrete appears, but in which everything hangs on the here and now, can exist in pure and God-directed form. Only when we are sure that this moment of the real presence exists in the human being who experiences it, can we then ask the question whether it is or is not a true revelation—a moment not just of faith but of knowledge, and a gift of Grace.

Confronting the Skeptic

I will return to the topic of the sacred. But those few remarks prompt observations that will be important for my argument in the next two chapters. There are, it seems to me, two ways in to the topic of theology: the cosmological and the psychological. We can speculate about the nature and origin of the world, in search of the Being upon whom the natural order depends. And we can speculate about

[17] See Paul Ricoeur, *Figuring the Sacred: Religion, Narrative, and the Imagination*, ed. Mark I. Wallace, trans. David Pellauer (Minneapolis, MN: Augsburg Fortress, 1995).

the experience of holiness, in which individuals encounter another order of things, an intrusion into the natural world from a sphere "beyond" it. Both ways point toward the supernatural. There could not be an explanation of the world as a whole in natural terms since the explanation must reach beyond the realm of nature to its transcendental ground. There could not be an account of holiness—of the "numinous"—that did not relate the experience to a transcendental subject. The experience of sacred things is, I have suggested, a kind of interpersonal encounter. It is as though you address, and are addressed by, another I, but one that has no embodiment in the natural order. Your experience "reaches beyond" the empirical realm, to a place on its horizon. This idea is vividly conveyed in the Upanishads, in which Brahman, the creative principle, is represented as transcendental, universal, and also as *atman*, the self in which all our separate selves aspire to be absorbed and united.

The skeptical response to those observations is to say that they are both illusions. It is an illusion that the natural world has some other explanation than itself. For what is explanation, if not the demonstration that some phenomenon belongs in the natural order, the order of cause and effect as this is explored by science? It is an illusion that there are sacred things, sacred moments, holy mysteries. For we explain such things as we explain everything else, by showing their place in the order of nature. These experiences arise from the pressure of social life, which causes us to read intention, reason, and desire into all that surrounds us so that, finding no human cause for those things that most deeply affect us, we imagine a divine cause instead.

If we are to take seriously the argument of Kant in the *Critique of Pure Reason*, and that of Hume in the *Dialogues of Natural Religion*, then surely we have no choice but to accept that the two ways to the transcendental—the cosmological and the psychological—are both effectively blocked. We cannot, for reasons made clear by Kant, reason beyond the limits of our own point of view, which is circumscribed by the law of causality, and by the forms of space and time. We have no access to the transcendental perspective from which the question of the ultimate ground of reality can be meaningfully asked, let alone answered. And we cannot, for reasons made clear by Hume, deduce from our religious experiences that they are not illusions. To understand religious experiences, we should not look at them from the first-person point of view, but from outside—as though they were the experiences of others. And we should look for the natural explanation, the one that would appeal to us, were we trying to understand, as an anthropologist might, the customs of a foreign tribe. We might arrive at the conclusion that the experience of the sacred is a vital adaptation, like the horror of incest. But this does nothing to justify the perspective of the religious believer, for whom this experience is a window onto the transcendental and an encounter with the hidden God.

I share that skepticism, up to a point. But it does not satisfy me, and I shall briefly state the reason here. Kant is right in his claim that scientific knowledge shows the world from our point of view—the point of view of "possible experience"—and as bounded by space, time, and causality. He is also right, however, that reason is tempted to reach beyond those boundaries, striving to grasp the world as a whole and from a transcendental perspective. Kant believed that this temptation leads to contradictions, some of which he exposed in the "Antinomies" chapter of the *Critique of Pure Reason*. His greatest successor, Hegel, denied that those contradictions set limits to rational inquiry. Reason, for Hegel, is constantly transcending its own partial viewpoints, on its journey toward the "Absolute Idea." Reason aims of its nature toward a kind of final narrative of how things are, in which all the contradictions (which are contradictions only from a partial perspective) are overcome. If Hegel is right, then the cosmological path points beyond the edge of the world as science describes it, to a place where another kind of question can be asked, a question that cannot be answered with a cause, but only with a reason: the question "why?" asked of the world as a whole—the question addressed to Brahman. We can answer such a question only by giving a teleological, rather than a causal, account of things. That account will make no difference to, and have no contact with, cosmological science.

Undoubtedly, from the scientific point of view, religious beliefs and practices are not to be explained as the pious would wish. The two centuries of skeptical reasoning, from Diderot and Hume through Feuerbach and Renan to the evolutionary psychologists today, must alert us to the evident truth that religion is a natural phenomenon like any other, to be explained first in terms of its social and evolutionary function and second in terms of things going on in the brain of the believer. Of course religions offer a powerful narrative of past events and unseen presences, through which to endow the trivial matter of our species life with a goal and a meaning. It is through these fictions that people understand the experience of sacred things. But the fictions neither explain the experience nor justify its intrinsic claim to veracity.

Yet here too there is more to be said. Of course there are idolatrous religions and religions that muddle the natural and the supernatural in ways that make nonsense of both. But there are also religions that turn their backs on idolatrous practices, that invite us to address the specific moments of ritual involvement with an alertness that reaches precisely beyond what is present to the senses, toward the perspective lying on the edge of things, which addresses us I to I. The narrative of a religion is like a commentary on these moments, a prop to be discarded when the experience, the *sakīnah*, has been fully grasped. This "reaching beyond" of the religious moment is not different, I shall suggest, from the transcendental urge of reason itself. Ultimately the cosmological and the psychological paths are paths toward the same destination, and that destination lies on the far horizon of our world.

2

Looking for People

My argument so far has concerned a set of difficult notions that are not always given a central role in religious experience: notions of the sacred, the real presence, and the search in this world for God. Whatever we think of the evolutionary significance of religious belief, and its role in natural selection, we should recognize that there is another and far more transparent function that religion seems to perform: the maintenance of the life of the person. Every aspect of religious belief and obedience contributes to this. Religions focus and amplify the moral sense; they ring-fence those aspects of life in which personal responsibilities are rooted—notably sex, family, territory, and law. They feed into the distinctively human emotions, like hope and charity, which lift us above the motives that rule the lives of other animals, and cause us to live by culture and not by instinct.

Some people object to religion precisely on these grounds—namely, that faith invades the moral sphere and in some way overrides its inbuilt claim to our obedience. What is most objectionable about religion, in the vision of the humanists, is the attempt to capture in God's name the moral resources on which we humans depend. Thus in Feuerbach's view Christianity confiscates our virtues and projects them into an inaccessible realm of heavenly beings, so alienating us from our own moral life.[1] However, the criticism cuts both ways. In the hands of Wagner, Feuerbach's vision of the gods, as projections of our mortal passions, acquired a new and redemptive significance. Only what is already spiritually transcendent, Wagner's music suggests, can be projected in this way onto the screen of Valhalla. Because the gods live from our moral sentiments, they are redeemed

[1]Ludwig Feuerbach, *The Essence of Christianity*, trans. George Eliot, new ed. (Cambridge: Cambridge University Press, 2011).

through us and dependent upon our sacrificial passions. And those passions contain their moral value within themselves. Religion does not detract from the redemptive power of our emotions, but endows the moral life with a narrative that reveals its inner truth.[2]

The Concept of the Person

Gods are not things, nor even animals, though they may show themselves in animal guise like the gods of the ancient Egyptians. A god is the object of a personal encounter. It is thus that Isis reveals herself to Apuleius in *The Golden Ass*. Even the metaphysical religions of the East place the personal encounter at the heart of their rituals and observances. The avatars of Shiva and Krishna patrol the streets of the Hindu cities, and Krishna reveals himself to Arjuna, in the *Baghavad Gita*, offering very personal advice about the responsibilities incurred in battle. Krishna speaks in the person of Arjuna's charioteer, but he is also speaking for Brahman, the Eternal One, and is concerned to reinforce the view that we have no model, in our human understanding, with which to conceive this being from whom all proceeds and on whom all depends, except that of the self—described as the *atman*, using the Sanskrit reflexive pronoun. The burden of the *Gita* is that we must devote our lives to the Supreme Being. Everything that we do to give consciousness priority over matter, to give power to the real self within, by releasing it from all concern with temporal and sensory things, will bring us closer to the universal self, the Brahman, which is our final haven and place of rest. The doctrine resembles Saint Augustine's view, that we are restless until we rest in Christ, and Saint Paul's vision of the Holy Spirit parallels that expressed at 9:28 of the *Gita*: "those who worship me with devotion (*yoga*) dwell in me, and I too in them." Throughout the *Gita*, indeed, we find the two paths to the divine—the cosmological and the psychological—wrapped constantly into one, as the inner knowledge of self is reworked as an outer knowledge of the divine principle from which

---

[2]See R. Wagner, "Die Religion und die Kunst," in *Gesammelte Schriften und Dichtungen*, 2nd ed. (Leipzig: Fritzsch, 1887–88), 10:211.

the world of contingencies flows. The search for the foundation of the world is the search for the I that looks down on us from a point outside time.

Likewise the Buddhists, when the chips are down, declare that they "take refuge in the Buddha, in the *dharma* (precepts) and in the *sangha* (sacred community)," suggesting that a kind of personal devotion takes precedence over *nirvana* even in this, the most impersonal of all the major faiths. In all its forms religion involves a beseeching of the unknown to reveal itself as both object and subject of love. To look for God is to look for the redeeming person, to whom you can entrust your life.

The term "person" comes to us from Latin *persona*, which originally referred to the theatrical mask, and hence to the character who spoke through it. The term was taken up by the Roman law to denote the right-and-duty bearing subject of the law. And it found a home in philosophy, when Boethius defined "person" as "an individual substance of a rational nature," suggesting that a person is *essentially* a person, and therefore could not cease to be a person without ceasing to be. Aquinas took up this definition and recognized that it confers on us another essence than that conferred by membership of a biological species. Thus arose the problem, already acknowledged by Aquinas but made famous by Locke, of personal identity. Could a person have a different history from the human organism in which he is embodied? A cloud of thought experiments have rushed like maddened insects from the corpse of Locke's problem, and there is no way of shutting them back, now that the corpse has decomposed.

More important for present purposes is the reworking of the concept of the person in the philosophy of Kant and Hegel. In Kant the idea of the "individual substance" takes second place, and reason steps forward to replace it. The crucial feature of the rational being for Kant is not substantial unity or the capacity to follow arguments, but self-consciousness and the use of "I." It is because I can identify myself in the first person that I am able to live the life of the rational being, and this fact situates me in the web of interpersonal relations from which the basic precepts of morality derive. (See especially Kant's lectures published as *Anthropology from a Pragmatic Viewpoint*.) The self-identifying subject is both transcendentally free and endowed with the "transcendental unity of apperception"—the immediate knowledge of self as a unified center of consciousness.

Those ideas demand exposition in more modern terms; and the same is true of the additions to the Kantian picture made by Hegel. For Hegel persons *achieve* the freedom and self-consciousness that distinguish them, and the process of acquiring these attributes is one that winds us into relations of submission and domination with others of our kind and also leads us on to the point of both claiming and according the recognition on which the moral order is founded. I come to know myself as subject through a process of self-alienation, whereby I encounter myself from outside, so to speak, as an object among others. I must seize my freedom from the world of strangers and competitors, by compelling others to recognize that I am indeed free and therefore to be treated not as a means, as objects are treated, but as an end. In the dialectical process whereby freedom comes into being, we exchange relations of power for relations of right, and solipsistic appetites for a life negotiated with others. Hegel's masterly and poetic description of this process[3] has had a lasting influence on philosophy and again demands to be described in more modern terms. In particular, we must show how the dialectic, which Hegel presents in narrative form, is not a process in time, but the internal logic of our states of mind: a process that exists only in the product.

Understanding and Explaining

We should begin from the first-person case, since it is misunderstandings concerning the sense of "I" that have led to the most influential mistakes about its reference—including the mistake of Descartes, who believed that the first-person pronoun refers to a nonphysical and nonspatial substance revealed directly only to itself. One thing is immediately apparent, and this is that many statements made in the first-person case are epistemologically privileged. When I say I am in pain, wanting to leave the room, thinking of Elizabeth, or worried

---

[3] See especially *The Phenomenology of Spirit* (1807), chap. titled "Self-Consciousness," subsection "Lordship and Bondage."

about my son, then I am reporting states of affairs about which I cannot, in the normal case, be mistaken, and concerning which I do not have to find out whether they obtain. This epistemological privilege seems to be bound up, in some way, with the *grammar* of the first-person case: someone who didn't use the word "I" to make privileged claims of this kind would show that he hadn't understood it. Self-consciousness presupposes the privileges of first-person awareness, and the existence of these privileges is also assumed in our interpersonal dialogue.

"I" is an indexical term, like "here" and "now." However, this does not explain the epistemological peculiarities to which I have just referred. Although there is a sense in which I cannot mistakenly identify the place where I am as here, and the time at which I am speaking as now, I have no special privilege as to what is going on here and now, other than those privileges that depend on my use of "I." On the other hand, it is clear that there is no place for indexical terms in science, and that, just as a unified science must replace all reference to "here" and "now" with positions identified in four-dimensional space, so must it drop the use of "I." As Thomas Nagel has pointed out, however, this leads to a singular puzzle concerning the relation between myself and the world.[4] We can imagine a scientific description of the world, which identifies all the particles and fields of force, all the laws of motion that govern their changes, and which gives a complete identification of the positions of everything at some given time. But, however complete this description might be, there is one fact that it does not mention and which is, for me, the most important fact there is, namely, which of the objects in this world am I? Where am I, in the world of unified science? The identification of any object in the first-person case is ruled out by the enterprise of scientific explanation. So science cannot tell me who I am, let alone where, when, or how.

Nevertheless, we should not deceive ourselves into thinking that people have a purely "subjective" existence, which removes them in some way from the spatiotemporal continuum. We are persons; but persons are also objects that we come across in the world of our

---

[4]See Thomas Nagel, *The View from Nowhere* (New York: Oxford University Press, 1986).

perception. Persons act on and are acted on by other objects, and there are laws that govern their coming into being and their passing away.

Persons are therefore objects; but they are also subjects. They identify themselves in the first person, and this way of identifying themselves is an immovable part of the ways in which we describe them. A person is, for us, a someone, and not just a something.[5] Persons are able to reply to the question "why?" asked of their state, their beliefs, their intentions, their plans, and their desires. This means that, while we often endeavor to explain people in the way we explain other objects in our environment—in terms of cause and effect, laws of motion, and physical makeup—we also have another kind of access to their past and future conduct. In addition to *explaining* their behavior, we seek to *understand* it; and the contrast between explaining and understanding is pertinent to our whole way of describing persons and their world.

The distinction here can be traced to Kant's arguments concerning practical reason, and to the Kantian theology of Schleiermacher. But modern discussions typically begin from Wilhelm Dilthey, and the theory of *Verstehen*.[6] According to Dilthey rational agents look on the world in two contrasting (though not necessarily conflicting) ways: as something to be explained, predicted, and brought under universal laws; and as an occasion for thought, action, and emotion. When looking on the world in the latter way, as an object of our attitudes, emotions, and choices, we understand it through the conceptions that we use of each other, when engaged in justifying and influencing our conduct. We look for reasons for action, meanings, and appropriate occasions of feeling. We are not explaining the world in terms of physical causes, but *interpreting* it as an object of our personal responses. Our explanations seek the reason rather than the cause; and our descriptions are also invocations and modes of address.

Dilthey's thesis is both difficult to state and controversial; and it is fair to say that he himself never explained it with the clarity that we

---

[5] See Robert Spaemann, *Persons: On the Difference between Someone and Something*, trans. Oliver Donovan (Oxford: Oxford University Press, 2006).

[6] See especially W. Dilthey, *The Formation of the Historical World in the Human Sciences*, in *Selected Works*, ed. R. A. Makkreel and F. Rodi, vol. 3 (Princeton, NJ: Princeton University Press, 2002). The best introduction that I have found to Dilthey is the entry under his name in the *Stanford Encyclopedia of Philosophy*, available free online.

might reasonably demand. An example must, at this point, suffice. Imagine a fight to the death between two groups of people, in which one side is finally victorious. Having killed the enemy, the victors return home carrying the armor of the defeated, which they set up on an altar, around which they light lamps that they keep burning day and night thereafter. Why are they doing this? You can imagine an explanation in terms of the search for territory, and the disarming of those who compete for it. But all such biological explanations leave the central fact in a certain measure mysterious. Why are they treating the armor of their enemies in this way? The answer is that, for them, the armor is a *trophy*. This concept belongs to the reasoning with which they might justify their actions to each other. It clarifies what they are doing by answering the question "why?" And it conveys a reason that is an object of immediate knowledge in the minds of the soldiers themselves. The concept of the trophy belongs to *Verstehen*. It does not denote a property of the object that could figure in any physical science of its nature; but it brings that object into connection with the reasons, desires, and motives of the agents who are putting it to a use.

Verstehen should not be seen simply as an alternative way of conceptualizing the world—though it is that. It is a way of conceptualizing the world that emerges from our interpersonal dialogue. It is when addressing you as an I like me that I describe the world in terms of the useful, the beautiful, and the good, that I deck out the deliverances of the senses in emotional colors, that I draw your attention to things under such descriptions as graceful, delicate, tragic, and serene. In science we describe the world to others; in *Verstehen* we describe the world *for* others, and mold it according to the demands of the I-You encounter, on which our personal lives depend. To use an idiom of Husserl's, *Verstehen* is directed toward the *Lebenswelt*, the world of life, a world that is open to action, and organized by the concepts that shape our deeds.

In a now-famous article of analytical philosophy,[7] Wilfrid Sellars distinguished the "manifest image" of the world—the image represented in our perceptions and in the reasons and motives that govern

---

[7] "Philosophy and the Scientific Image of Man," in *Science, Perception and Reality* (Austin, TX: Ridgeview, 1963).

our response to it—from the "scientific image," which is the account that emerges through the systematic attempt to explain what we observe. The two images are not commensurate—there is no one-to-one correspondence between them, and features that belong to the manifest image may disappear from science. Thus colors and other secondary qualities, which belong to the way we perceive the world, do not feature as such in the theories of physics, which refers instead to the wavelengths of refracted light. In subsequent writings Sellars distinguished the space of law, in which events are represented according to the laws of physics, from the space of reasons, in which events are represented according to the norms of justification and reasoning that govern human action. These ideas have been taken up and elaborated in more recent work by John McDowell and Robert Brandom, and I suspect that much that I have to say will find an echo in their writings.[8] However, I believe that the distinction made by Sellars does not get to the heart of our predicament as subjects—that there is, underlying his account of the "manifest image," an insufficient theory of the first-person case and its role in interpersonal dialogue. I shall therefore proceed along the path that seems more immediately promising to me, taking note of Sellars and his followers from time to time, but bypassing their specific arguments. In particular I shall use Husserl's idiom, and refer to the *Lebenswelt*, rather than the manifest image, partly because I want to emphasize that the distinction between the world of science and the world in which we live is as much a matter of practical reason as perception.

Cognitive Dualism

In one respect, however, I shall follow Sellars. I shall develop a kind of cognitive dualism, according to which the world can be understood in two incommensurable ways, the way of science, and the way of interpersonal understanding. There are other precedents in philosophy

[8] John McDowell, *Mind and World* (Cambridge, MA: Harvard University Press, 1994); Robert Brandom, *Reason in Philosophy: Animating Ideas* (Cambridge, MA: Harvard University Press, 2009).

for the kind of suggestion that I wish to develop. Spinoza was perhaps the first to argue that the world is *one* thing, seen in two (*at least* two) distinct ways.[9] Thought and extension were, for Spinoza, two attributes of a single unified reality. Both delivered a complete form of knowledge: we could know the world as extension, through the study of physics. And through this study we would know, eventually, all that there is to be known. But the resulting science would make no mention of ideas, or of the mind as their vehicle. Likewise, through the study of ideas, we could know the world as thought, and through this study too we would come to know all that is to be known. But the two studies would be incommensurable. We could no more pass from one to the other and back again than we could pass from a description of a painted face to a description of colored patches and back again, expecting thereby to give a complete account of a picture. The analogy with pictures is imperfect: but it helps us to see how what is one thing when viewed as a whole might nevertheless be understood in detail in two incommensurable ways.[10]

Kant's approach is similar. Our world, he argues, can be seen from the point of view of the understanding, in which case we know it as a web of causal connections laid out in space and time and subject to universal and necessary laws. But certain items within that world can be seen, and indeed must be seen, in another way, from the perspective of practical reason. That which, from the point of view of the understanding, is subject to biological laws that determine its behavior is, from the point of view of practical reason, a free agent, obedient to the laws of reason. These two points of view are incommensurable: that is to say, we cannot derive from one of them a description of the world as seen from the other. Nor can we understand how one and the same object can be apprehended from both perspectives. Indeed, it might be more correct to say that the thing which the understanding sees as an object, reason sees as a subject, and that the mysterious identity of subject and object is something that we know to obtain, even though we cannot understand *how* it

---

[9] I pass over the question whether Spinoza thought that God had *infinitely many* attributes, of which only two are known to us: see the discussion in my *Spinoza: A Very Short Introduction* (Oxford: Oxford University Press, 1986).

[10] On the relevance of the analogy to Spinoza, see ibid.

obtains, since we have no perspective that allows us to grasp both subject and object in a single mental act.

Cognitive dualism, whether of the Spinozist or the Kantian kind, is puzzling.[11] For it seems to be both affirming and denying the unity of reality, both affirming and denying that we human beings are part of the natural order. Yet we can without contradiction accept some version of it, provided we recognize the *explanatory* priority of science. To describe the "order of nature" in terms of some complete and unified science is to give a systematic answer to the question "what exists?" But the world can be known in another way, through the practice of *Verstehen*. The world known in this other way will be an "emergent" world, represented in the cognitive apparatus of the perceiver, but emerging *from* the physical reality, as the face emerges from the pigments on the canvas, or the melody from the sequence of pitched sounds. The relation of "emergence" is nonsymmetrical. The order of nature does not emerge from the *Lebenswelt*; it is, we might say, using an idiom of Strawson's, "ontologically prior": its existence is presupposed by the *Lebenswelt*, but not vice versa.[12]

From this arises the belief that the order of nature is *all that there really is*. But to draw that conclusion would be a mistake, for two reasons. First, the *Lebenswelt* is irreducible. We understand and relate to it using concepts of agency and accountability that have no place in the physical sciences; to use the idiom of Sellars, the *Lebenswelt* exists in "the space of reasons," not in "the space of law." Second, those concepts of agency and accountability extend their reach beyond the horizon of nature, so as to pose the question that science cannot formulate—the question "why?" asked of the world as a whole. This question opens the possibility that the order of nature is in its turn dependent. Nature does not stand in need of a causal explanation, but maybe it stands in need of a reasoned account.

An example is useful here. Consider the simple theme that opens Beethoven's Third Piano Concerto (ex. 1). From the point of view

---

[11] And there is another form of it, no less puzzling, described by Donald Davidson as "anomalous monism." See "Mental Events," in *Essays on Actions and Events*, 2nd ed. (Oxford: Clarendon Press, 2001).

[12] See chap. 1 of Strawson's *Individuals* (London: Routledge, 1956).

Ex. 1. Beethoven's Third Piano Concerto, opening.

of science this consists of a series of pitched sounds, one after the other, each identified by frequency. But we do not hear a sequence of pitched sounds. We hear a melody, which begins on the first note and moves upward from C to G, via E-flat, and then stepwise downward to the starting point. But somehow the movement hasn't stopped, and Beethoven decides to nail it down with two emphatic dominant-tonic commas. Then comes an answering phrase, harmonized this time, and leading up to A-flat construed as a dissonant minor ninth on G. We hear a sudden increase in tension, and a strong gravitational force pulling that A-flat downward on to G, although the melody doesn't rest there, since it is looking for the answer to the two dominant-tonic commas that we heard earlier, and it finds this answer in another pair of such commas, though this time in the key of G.

You could go on describing these few bars for a whole book, and you won't have exhausted all that they contain by way of musical significance. The point I want to emphasize, however, is that you cannot describe what is going on in this theme without speaking of movement in musical space, of gravitational forces, of answering phrases and symmetries, of tension and release, and so on. In describing the *music*, you are not describing *sounds* heard in a sequence; you are describing a kind of action in musical space, in which things move up and down in response to each other and against resisting fields of force. These fields of force order the one-dimensional space of music, in something like the way gravity orders the spatiotemporal continuum. In describing pitched sounds as music, we are situating them in another order of events than the order of nature.[13]

An expert in acoustics could give you a complete account of this theme—an account that would enable you to reproduce it by following his instructions—without mentioning or even hearing movement in musical space. Such an expert would describe sequences of pitched sounds, not musical tones. The acoustician and the musical listener apprehend what they hear in two different ways. Each way is cognitively complete—that is to say, it apprehends and orders everything that is there. And the two ways are incommensurable, in the sense that a partial apprehension under one of them cannot be completed by a partial apprehension under the other. A description of the theme which tells us that it rises through an ascending minor triad from C to G, and then is succeeded by a sound one-third of the duration of the previous sound at pitch 349.2 hertz *breaks off* what was being described (the movement in musical space) and goes off in another direction (the direction required by the order of nature, which is an order of pitched sounds). There is a parallel here with pictures. You can describe a picture fully in terms of its represented subject, which is *seen in* the distribution of colored patches. But you cannot switch from a partial description of the subject matter to a description of pixels on a two-dimensional graph and back again, and still be describing what is seen.

This incommensurability extends even to the basic objects described. What from the acoustical point of view is one thing might, from the musical point of view, be two. Thus in a keyboard fugue two voices may coincide on a single pitch, creating a single sound. But in this single sound we hear two distinct tones, moving in two directions and belonging to two melodic lines. Conversely, what is acoustically plural (a collection of simultaneous pitches) might be musically singular (a chord). This is very obvious in the Beethoven example, where a chordal passage answers a passage of unisons and

---

[13] The space that I am invoking here is a phenomenological space, not a "geometry"—i.e., it is not simply a mapping of musical events onto points on a continuum. Such a mapping is possible—see, for example, Dmitri Tymoczko, *A Geometry of Music* (New York: Oxford University Press, 2010). But its existence says nothing about what we hear in hearing music. See my review of Tymoczko in *Reason Papers* (2012). I give a fuller account of musical space in *The Aesthetics of Music* (Oxford: Oxford University Press, 1997).

octaves, so that we hear the chords as musical individuals, in just the way that we hear the tones that precede them.

Now someone who wished to design a machine capable of delivering Beethoven's concerto to the ear, would not be helped by a description of the movement in musical space. But he would be helped by an analysis of the pitches and their duration. He could transcribe this analysis into a suitable digital notation and use the result to program a device capable of producing pitched sounds in sequence. And the device would be able to deliver to listeners just what they would hear when listening in the concert hall. Indeed, this is what happens with the art of recording. Someone could be a brilliant recording engineer, even though he was tone-deaf, hearing in music only sequences of pitched sounds. The reductivist would argue that therefore the music is *nothing but* the sequence of pitched sounds, since if you reproduce the sequence, you reproduce the music. The response is to say—sure, the music depends upon, is emergent from, the sequence of sounds. The sounds are "ontologically prior." But to hear the music it is not enough to notice the sounds. Music is inaudible, except to those with the cognitive capacity to hear movement in musical space, orientation, tension and release, the gravitational force of the bass notes, the goal directedness and action-profile of melodies, and so on. These things that we hear in music are not illusions: someone who fails to hear them does not hear all that there is to hear, just as someone who fails to see the face in a picture fails to see all that is there. Music is certainly part of the real world. But it is perceivable only to those who are able to conceptualize and respond to sound in ways that have no part to play in the physical science of acoustics.

It is helpful at this point to register a protest against what Mary Midgley calls "nothing buttery." There is a widespread habit of declaring emergent realities to be "nothing but" the things in which we perceive them. The human person is "nothing but" the human animal; law is "nothing but" relations of social power; sexual love is "nothing but" the urge to procreation; altruism is "nothing but" the dominant genetic strategy described by Maynard Smith;[14] the *Mona Lisa* is

---

[14] See J. Maynard Smith, "Group Selection and Kin Selection," *Nature* 201 (1964): 1145–47, and the same author's *Evolution and the Theory of Games* (Cambridge: Cambridge University Press, 1982).

"nothing but" a spread of pigments on a canvas, the Ninth Symphony is "nothing but" a sequence of pitched sounds of varying timbre. And so on. Getting rid of this habit is, to my mind, the true goal of philosophy. And if we get rid of it when dealing with the small things—symphonies, pictures, people—we might get rid of it when dealing with the large things too: notably, when dealing with the world as a whole. And then we might conclude that it is just as absurd to say that the world is nothing but the order of nature, as physics describes it, as to say that the *Mona Lisa* is nothing but a smear of pigments. Drawing that conclusion is the first step in the search for God.

Let us now return to the case of persons. The ontological dualism of Descartes survived into recent times as the view that consciousness could not be reduced to any physical process, and that the relation between the human brain and the human mind could not be deciphered or eliminated by any purely biological science. Always consciousness would be "left over" from any purely physical account of human thought and action, and its peculiar immediacy and transparency would be a kind of irreducible residue of neurological explanation. The reasons for maintaining this position were many; but the two most important were first-person phenomenology and intentionality. Introspection, the dualists argued, reveals an irreducible inner character to our mental states, a *quale*, that cannot be accounted for by any physical theory. Moreover, mental states have the peculiar feature of "directedness" or "aboutness," which cannot be reduced to any relation between physical events or things, but is entirely sui generis and a mark of the mental as such.

Qualia

Neither of those considerations, it seems to me, is sufficient to justify ontological dualism of the Cartesian kind. The first overlooks two important facts: that consciousness is distinct from self-consciousness, and that self-consciousness is not consciousness of a special kind of object. It is evident that consciousness is distinct from self-consciousness—consider the case of nonhuman animals, many of which are conscious, but few if any of which are self-conscious. We cannot account for the behavior of dogs and cats if we do not allow that they have perceptions, sensations, and also cognitive and appetitive attitudes. All these are conscious states—by which we mean that they involve awareness of the creature's condition and environment. Yet there is no room in our explanations of such creatures for the inner "whatness" or *quale* of their mental states, and while, with Thomas Nagel, we might raise the question what it is like to be a bat, there is no answer to be given in terms of *qualia*.[15] What Wittgenstein would call the "grammar" of "what it is like" works in another way. The phrase does not denote a publicly inaccessible quality of an experience; it summarizes what we know in having an experience, and what we imagine in imagining it. "What it's like" refers to "knowledge by acquaintance," and to "know what it's like" to swallow a snail is to have swallowed a snail.[16] It is not the special inner feel, the battiness, of the bat's experience that would tell us what it is like to be a bat. It is the bat's *form of life*, which we know by observation, but in which we cannot participate. We know that dogs feel pain, and that this experience is bad and an appropriate occasion for pity and rescue. But we have no grounds for supposing that there is anything going on in the injured dog beyond what is observable to the eye of science: pain is something that we can see, just as we see joy, depression, and desire.

The idea of the inner "whatness" or *quale* gains purchase only from the case of *self*-consciousness—the consciousness of creatures who, like me, can *say* what they are feeling, and who have an immediate and criterionless awareness of their own mental state. It is the existence of this "subjective point of view," enshrined in the use of "I," and in the first-person attribution of mental states, that gives rise to the belief that there is something *else* to a mental state than what can be discovered by physical means. In my own case, it is argued, I am presented with the inner process *as it is in itself*, and this shows me something that can never be observed by another, for the very reason that it is available only to introspection.

[15] See "What Is It Like to Be a Bat?" in *Mortal Questions* (Oxford: Oxford University Press, 1982).

[16] See my discussion of this point in *Art and Imagination* (London: Methuen, 1974), pp. 105–6.

That view of the first-person case was patiently and, in my view, definitively demolished by Wittgenstein in *Philosophical Investigations*, though already in the "Paralogisms" chapter of the *Critique of Pure Reason* Kant had pointed to the fallacy involved in construing self-consciousness as consciousness of a certain kind of *object* that stands apart from the other objects in our shared physical world. It is true that each person has privileged knowledge of his own present state of mind, and is immediately aware of a whole range of mental states that he can attribute to himself on no basis. The illusion persists that therefore there is some special fact about those mental states, an inner glow, as it were, revealed only to him, which he is able to record because it is immediately present to his consciousness in a way that no physical object or event could be present. Furthermore, it is supposed, this inner *quale* is precisely what is *mental* about each mental state. Hence, on this view, the "inner life" is *essentially* inner: unobservable to others and conducted in a world of its own.

To dispel those illusions is not easy. But their illusory character is made beautifully apparent by Wittgenstein in the sections of *Philosophical Investigations* sometimes known as the "private language argument."[17] The conclusion to be drawn from those sections is that first-person knowledge of the mental is knowledge on *no basis*; a fortiori it is not knowledge of something unobservable to others. The mind is out there and observable; but to observe it we must use other concepts, and make other connections, than those used and made by the natural sciences.

To take that position is not to deny that our experiences have qualities, or that they can be qualitatively compared. We attribute qualities to many of our experiences not by looking inward, but by looking outward, at the secondary qualities of objects. Seeing red is a distinct visual experience; but to describe that experience is to describe how red things look, which in turn requires an act of ostension. Red

---

[17] Ludwig Wittgenstein, *Philosophical Investigations* (Oxford: Oxford University Press, 1952), pt. 1, secs. 220 et seq. I offer a version of the argument in chap. 4 of *Modern Philosophy* (London: Sinclair-Stevenson, 1994). See also the strongly argued denial of *qualia* given by Michael Tye, *Consciousness, Color, and Content* (Cambridge, MA: MIT Press, 2000). For an overview of the now prodigiously abundant literature on *qualia*, see Michael Tye's article under that heading in the *Stanford Encyclopedia of Philosophy*, online.

things are things that look like *this*; and seeing red is a visual experience you have when you see something that looks like *this*. Seeing red is distinct from seeing green, because red things are distinct from green things. Undeniably, that raises the question of secondary qualities—are they really there, *in* the things that seem to possess them? I incline to the view that secondary qualities are dispositions to elicit experiences in the normal observer, but that the experiences must in turn be identified through the qualities of the things that we perceive. The circularity of such an account is, to my mind, a benign and not a vicious circularity.[18] Meanwhile, we should note that, for many mental states, there *is* no "what it's like" to be in them. There is nothing that it's like to believe that carbon dioxide is a gas, to wonder whether the moon is made of cheese, to admire Jane rather than Mary, to doubt Justin's evidence, to understand Pascal's theorem, or to read this sentence. Yet those mental states are as much part of the inner life as sensations and perceptions.

Intentionality

Those arguments, it seems to me, destroy the grounds for thinking of consciousness as a peculiar residue, an inner glow that is somehow attached to events and processes that can otherwise be described in the language and theories that describe physical reality. More tricky, however, is the second argument for a deep ontological dualism: the argument from intentionality. This argument so impressed Brentano that, having set it out at the beginning of his book purporting to outline "psychology from an empirical standpoint," he found himself unable to proceed further. For it seemed to pose an insuperable obstacle to any empirical investigation of psychological states. (See *Psychology from an Empirical Standpoint*, vol. 1—vol. 2 never appeared.) To put the point simply, mental states—or at any rate an all-important and central set of them—are *about* things other than themselves, and

---

[18] See the argument about sounds in Scruton, *The Aesthetics of Music*, chap. 1. For interesting reflections on the way in which subjective experience and secondary qualities are mutually entwined, see Colin McGinn, *The Subjective View: Secondary Qualities and Indexical Thoughts* (Oxford: Oxford University Press, 1983), and Tye, *Consciousness, Color, and Content*.

this relation of aboutness seems to have no place in physical reality. I can think about what is nonexistent; I can want, imagine, and decide on things that have no conceivable place in the physical world or which, if they do exist there, may be entirely other than I think them to be. I can focus my mental states on objects that are indeterminate, even though everything real is determinate, and so on. So how can mental states be part of physical reality, when they are bound up with a relation of "aboutness" that cannot be securely fastened to the physical world?

Two fashionable responses to this question help to dissipate its urgency: those of Dennett and Searle.[19] Dennett argues that intentional idioms—such as those involved in ascribing beliefs, desires, and intentions—have an *explanatory* role. We can explain the behavior of an organism more easily if we conceptualize its behavior in this way, and in so doing we take an "intentional stance" toward it, relating to it as we relate to each other, asking what it wants and thinks, and assuming that it in general wants what is good for it and thinks what is true. The possibility of adopting this intentional stance, Dennett suggests, in no way implies that we are dealing with a nonphysical object, or that the behavior that interests us could not be explained more mechanistically, or in terms of some computational process that is hidden from everyday view. After all, we can relate more easily to our computers if we describe them as thinking this, and wanting that; on Dennett's view we can even take an intentional stance to a thermostat, which "tries" to restore the temperature of a room when it "thinks" it is too hot, and so on.

The argument presupposes that the creature *taking* the intentional stance—the one who is able to interpret the world in this way, in terms of thought, perception, and desire—can himself be explained nonintentionally, that the "stance" is only a stance, and that every object toward which this stance is appropriate can be understood in another way, as a computational system. But those entities that can be so explained—thermostats and computers, for example—are

[19] Daniel C. Dennett, *The Intentional Stance* (Cambridge, MA: MIT Press, 1989); J. R. Searle, *Intentionality: An Essay in the Philosophy of Mind* (Cambridge: Cambridge University Press, 1983), and *Rationality in Action* (Cambridge, MA: MIT Press, 2001).

precisely those that we recognize to be *other* than us, machines onto which we are *projecting* our own mental equipment in what we know in our hearts to be an elaborate metaphor.

Hence we need a further argument, one that either eliminates the intentional stance entirely, or shows intentionality to be a property of physical systems. The second path is the one taken by Searle, and also by Fodor and other defenders of the "representational theory of mind." Their response is to grant that intentionality is a remarkable feature of the things that possess it, but to argue that this does not show that the things that possess it are not also *physical* things. Isn't a written sentence a physical thing? Cannot animals be in states of the nervous system, such that "aboutness" is reasonably ascribed to them? Indeed, isn't that what the nervous system is for? "About, my head," said Hamlet, thereby touching on the central feature of thinking—namely, that it is about the world, but goes on in the head.

It seems to me that this response is along the right lines, but that it opens the way to dualism of another kind, the dualism that I shall be defending. When I ascribe intentional states to a dog, it is by way of explaining its behavior. But of course, it is *we* who formulate the explanations, and who contribute the concepts used in framing them. Those concepts pick out objective features in the dog's environment, and classify them according to scientific principles that we understand, but which have no place in the thinking of a dog. A dog's beliefs and desires concern the world as it is presented to the dog's perception. The dog smells a hare, sees a man, and hears a horn. I can know this only because I identify those things in the dog's environment, and only because I know that he can react selectively to the smell of a *hare* (as opposed to, say, a rabbit), to the sight of a *man* (as opposed to, say, a scarecrow), to the sound of a horn (as opposed to, say, a violin). The use of these terms to describe the content of the dog's beliefs depends upon the causal relation between the dog's perceptual experience and the objects that surround him. I don't have to look to any inner "theater of consciousness" in order to describe the dog's beliefs; nor could I look for one. Whatever computational theory we develop, by way of explaining the passage from input to output in the mind of a dog, it is in terms of the physical world—the world that impacts upon the dog's perception—that the intentional content of the dog's state of mind will be described. To use the technical jargon, in accounting for the aboutness of animal minds, we take an "externalist" perspective. The dog's beliefs are beliefs *de re*, not *de dicto*: we identify them in terms of the things that *we* notice in the dog's environment, using concepts that belong to natural science.

Cognitive Dualism Again

Things are quite otherwise with us. As Searle has argued over many years and in many books, the human world contains things that do not exist independently of our intentional states, since they are brought into being by human declarations. Ours is a world of institutions, laws, and covenants. We are surrounded on every side by things that exist by fiat, and whose perpetuity depends upon our acquiescence. These things do not derive only from individual promises, enactments, and decrees; more importantly, Searle argues, they depend upon what he calls "social intentionality"—the shared sense that *we* are collectively under certain obligations. Human life could not be understood without reference to this kind of collective intentionality, which, according to Searle's plausible claim, creates "desire-independent reasons for action." The human world is an assemblage of "deontic powers," which pertain to offices, institutions, laws, and conventions that were brought into being, as contracts are brought into being, by our undertaking to respect them.[20]

In itself that thesis does not imply that human beings are to be understood in a completely different way from the way in which dogs are understood. Collective intentionality could be just as much a natural phenomenon, and just as easily subsumed under a unified science, as the intentionality of dogs, cats, and birds. However, there is a complication to which Searle, in my view, does not sufficiently attend. Human declarations—such as promises—are commitments made in the first-person case, often to another identified as "you." They are situated in the web of I-You encounters, and would be inconceivable without the peculiar privileges that attach to first-person knowledge.

[20] See J. R. Searle, *The Construction of Social Reality* (New York: Free Press, 1995); *Making the Social World: The Structure of Human Civilisation* (Oxford: Oxford University Press, 2009); etc.

The sign of intentional action is the ability of the agent to say immediately, and on no basis, that *this* is what he is doing, and to offer answers to the question "why?"[21] And intentions for the future are distinguished from predictions by the fact that those who declare them are prepared to offer first-person reasons for that which they resolve to do. Furthermore, as Searle and others have noted, intentions have a reflexive character. If I intend to do something, I do not merely intend that the thing should be done; I intend that it should be brought about by my intention. In expressing my intention, I make myself accountable for a future state of affairs: nonperformance requires a justification, and if my intention is expressed as part of a promise, then I owe it to the other to do what I have said.

Those and similar features mean that first-person awareness and accountability to the other are wound into our social intentionality. The states of mind that are directed toward the world of human covenants and institutions are directed toward a world of "I"s and "You"s, and are founded on the assumption that all participants in that world know immediately and on no basis not only what they intend but also their reasons (some of them, at least) for intending it. This assumption places a radical constraint upon the way in which the objects of social awareness can be conceptualized. I do not look on the other, still less on myself, as an organism, whose behavior is to be explained by some hypothesis concerning the nature of its intentional states. I look on the other as I look on myself—as an "I," whom I *address* in the second person, and whose self-attribution of reasons takes precedence, for me, over any third-person vision of what makes him tick.

This second-person standpoint has been discussed at length by Stephen Darwall, and has had a part to play in philosophy at least since the argument about lordship and bondage in Hegel's *Phenomenology of Spirit*. It features in Strawson's celebrated paper "Freedom and Resentment."[22] And it brings with it the suggestion that there are ways of conceptualizing people that, precisely because they respect the first-person case as having a special authority in our mutual

---

[21] The point has been subtly made by Elizabeth Anscombe, *Intention* (Oxford: Blackwell, 1957).

[22] Stephen Darwall, *The Second-Person Standpoint: Morality, Respect, and Accountability* (Cambridge, MA: Harvard University Press, 2006); P. F. Strawson, *Freedom and Resentment and Other Essays* (London: Taylor and Francis, 2008).

dealings, use concepts that have no role to play in the empirical sciences. When addressing my wife in interpersonal dialogue, I give precedence to her first-person avowals. The reasons that she offers me are the reasons that count, and her sincere declarations of intention and belief form the ground of my response to her. I see her as a free center of consciousness, who addresses me from the perspective of an "I" that is unified, individual, and unique as I am. When I ask her, "what are you going to do?" my question seeks a response. It is quite unlike the question "what is he going to do?" and the two questions do not feature here as substitution instances of a single schema, "what is x going to do?" One question is seeking a decision, the other a prediction, and in seeking a decision I am addressing the I in you. To do this, I commit myself to those "desire-independent reasons" to which Searle refers, and these reasons are shaped by concepts that have no part to play in the description of the physical world: concepts like right, duty, justice, virtue, purity, which inform our interpersonal exchanges.

Central to interpersonal dialogue is the practice of accountability. We hold each other to account, not only for our actions, but also for our thoughts, feelings, and attitudes. The question "why?" addressed from me to you, is not as a rule asking for an explanation, and certainly not for the kind of explanation that a neurologist might give. It is asking for an account of how things are, from your first-person perspective, that will render you intelligible, and in the normal case acceptable, to me. Sometimes you might be able to offer a justification for your actions and feelings. At other times your account of them will fall short of justifying them, but nevertheless acknowledge your accountability. (Think of a dialogue in which the first move is "Are you angry with me?")

So vivid and central in our lives is the I-You encounter that we are naturally tempted to believe that it is an encounter between objects, and that these objects exist in some other dimension from that containing ordinary physical things. It is this, I believe, rather than the mysteries of the "inner" life, that prompts people to espouse some kind of ontological dualism, and to believe that the human being is not one thing but two. I have suggested rather that there is a cognitive dualism, but not an ontological dualism, underlying our response to the human world. The I-You encounter is precisely not an encounter between objects, and therefore not an encounter between objects of a special and ontologically primitive kind. It is an encounter between subjects, and one that can be understood only if we recognize that the logic of first-person awareness is built into the concepts through which our mutual dealings are shaped.

Where in the world should we look for people, then? What I have suggested is that we are not looking for a special kind of object, but rather for an object to which we can respond in a special kind of way. The obvious candidates are human beings—members of the natural kind *Homo sapiens*, whose biological constitution defines the way they are. But then what of the first-person case? It is not essential to human beings that they identify themselves in the first person; yet it is essential to persons. First-person awareness is the premise of interpersonal relations, and it is on those relations that our nature as persons depends.

It is for this reason that we find the question of personal identity so puzzling. The philosophical literature abounds in thought experiments, from John Locke and Thomas Reid to Sydney Shoemaker and Derek Parfit, which remind us that the identity of the person and the identity of the body can be prized apart. And it seems odd to say that the person is identical with the human being, when the conditions that settle the identity of the one are distinct from those that settle the identity of the other. Maybe the case is more like that of the image and the canvas, or the melody and the sequence of sounds. Maybe we should say that a given person is *realized in* a given human being, rather than that he is *identical with* it—opening the possibility that one and the same person might be realized now in one body, now in another.

In that case, however, where exactly is the other person to be found? How do we discover his true nature? And what is the relevance of the human organism to our understanding of the person? Suppose you thought that the individual person existed in his body in something like the way a painted face exists in the pigments on the canvas. You would then be tempted to think that understanding the workings of the body was no more closely related to understanding the person than the chemical theory of pigments was to reading the meaning of the painted face. There would be a nonnavigable epistemological gap between our theory of the human being and our knowledge of the person. But is it really like that? What exactly follows from the kind of cognitive dualism that I have been advancing in this chapter?

3

■■■■■■■■

Looking at the Brain

When we consider nonhuman animals, it is hard to doubt that they receive information from their body and their environment, that this information is processed in some way by their central nervous system, of which the brain is the most important part, and that behavior issues as a result of this. When speaking of animal minds, therefore, we could as well be speaking of animal brains. And if this is true of animals, is it not also true of humans? Why should we resist that conclusion, once we have abandoned the ontological dualism that I rejected in the first two chapters?

In her highly influential book, *Neurophilosophy*, published in 1986, Patricia Churchland recommends that we ask ourselves just what philosophy has contributed to our understanding of human mental processes—just what, that is, compared to the extensive findings of neuroscience.[1] The answer is not much, or even nothing at all, depending on your level of exasperation. Churchland is of the view that philosophical arguments about our existing concepts—the concepts of "folk psychology," as she calls them—are of no real significance. It is not just that these arguments are "merely verbal," as was often said in the past. It is that they ignore the fact that our folk concepts belong to a theory—a useful theory, and one that gives us a handle on human language and human behavior—but a theory nevertheless. And theories get replaced by better ones. That, she tells us, is what is happening, as neuroscience takes over from folk psychology, providing better explanations of human behavior than could ever be obtained from that old-fashioned language of belief, perception, emotion, and desire. It is over twenty-five years since Churchland's book was published, and in

---

[1] Patricia Smith Churchland, *Neurophilosophy: Toward a Unified Science of the Mind-Brain* (Cambridge, MA: MIT Press, 1986).

the wake of it whole disciplines have sprung into being, proudly sporting the prefix "neuro-" by way of attaching themselves to Churchland's banner. We have entered a new period in which philosophy, once the handmaiden of theology, is seen by a substantial community of its practitioners as the handmaiden of neuroscience, whose role is to remove the obstacles that have been laid in the path of scientific advance by popular prejudice and superstitious ways of thinking.

On the other hand, the concept of the person, which has been a central concern of philosophy at least since the Middle Ages, resists translation into the idiom of neuroscience, being associated with ways of understanding and interpreting human beings that bypass causal laws and theory-building categories. As I argued in the previous chapter, we evaluate human conduct in terms of free choice and responsibility. Persons are singled out from the rest of our environment as recipients of love, affection, anger, and forgiveness. We face them eye to eye and I to I, believing each person to be a center of self-conscious reflection who responds to reasons, who makes decisions, and whose life forms a continuous narrative in which individual identity is maintained from moment to moment and from year to year. All those aspects of our interpersonal understanding are assumed in moral judgment, in the law, in religion, politics, and the arts. And all sit uneasily with the picture of our condition that is advocated by many students of neuroscience, who describe the supposedly distinctive features of humanity as adaptations, more sophisticated than the social skills to be observed in the other animals, but not fundamentally different in their origin or function. These adaptations, they suggest, are "hardwired" in the human brain, to be understood in terms of their function in the cognitive processing that occurs, when sensory inputs lead to behavioral outputs that have served the cause of reproduction. Moreover, the neuroscientists are likely to insist, the brain processes that are represented in our conscious awareness are only a tiny fragment of what is going on inside our heads. The "I," in David Eagleman's charming simile, is like a passenger, pacing the deck of a vast oceangoing liner, while persuading himself that he moves it with his feet.[2]

[2]David Eagleman, *Incognito: The Secret Lives of the Brain* (New York: Oxford University Press, 2011).

Brain-imaging techniques have been used to cast doubt on the reality of human freedom, to revise the description of reason and its place in human nature, and to question the validity of the old distinction of kind, which separated person from animal, and the free agent from the conditioned organism. And the more we learn about the brain and its functions, the more do people wonder whether our old ways of managing our lives and resolving our conflicts—the ways of moral judgment, legal process, and the imparting of virtue—are the best ways, and whether there might be more direct forms of intervention that would take us more speedily, more reliably, and maybe more kindly to the right result.

The nervous system is a network of yes/no switches, and the conviction is gaining ground that they function as "logic gates," the brain being a kind of digital computer, which operates by carrying out computations on information received through the many receptors located around the body, and delivering appropriate responses. This conviction is reinforced by research into artificial neural networks, in which the gates are connected so as to mimic some of the brain's capacities. Research into artificial intelligence connects directly with "cognitive science," a discipline that originally grew from the speculations launched by Alan Turing and others, when the idea of computation began to be widely studied by logicians. The major concern of the discipline is to understand the *kind* of link that is established between a creature and its environment, by the various "cognitive" processes, such as learning and perception.

In a creature with a mind, there is no direct law-like connection between sensory input and behavioral output. How the creature responds depends on what it perceives, what it desires, what it believes, and so on. Those states of mind involve truth-claims, and reference-claims, which are not explicable in mechanistic terms. Cognitive science must therefore show how truth-claims and reference-claims arise, and how they can be causally efficacious. Much of the resulting theory arises from a priori reflection, and without recourse to experiment. For instance, Fodor's well-known modular theory of the mind identifies discrete functions by reflecting on the nature of thought and on the connections between thought and action, and between thought and its objects in the world.[3] It says little about the brain, although it has been an inspiration to neuroscientists, many of whom have been guided by it in their search for discrete neural pathways and allocated areas of the cortex.

Evolutionary psychology tells us to look at the brain as the outcome of a process of adaptation. To understand what the brain is doing, we should ask how the genes of its owner would gain a competitive advantage by its doing just *this*, in the environment that originally shaped our species. For example: in what way did organisms steal a genetic march, in those long hard Pleistocene years, by reacting not to changes in their environment, but to changes in their own *thoughts* about the environment? In what way did they benefit genetically from a sense of beauty? And so on. I have already pointed out that much has been said by evolutionary psychologists concerning altruism, and how it might be explained as an "evolutionarily stable strategy." One kind of neuroscientist might be interested in taking up the point, arguing that altruism must therefore be "hardwired" in the brain, and that we should expect to find dedicated pathways and centers to which it can be assigned. Suppose you have proved that something called altruism is an evolutionarily stable strategy for organisms like us; and suppose that you have found the web of neurons that fire in your brain whenever you perform some altruistic act or gesture. Does that not say *something* at least about the workings of our moral emotions, and doesn't it also place severe limits on what a *philosopher* might say?

You can see from that example how the three disciplines of neurophysiology, cognitive science, and evolutionary psychology might converge, each taking a share in defining the questions and each taking a share in answering them. I want to urge a few doubts as to whether it is right to run these disciplines together, and also whether it is right to think that, by doing so, we cast the kind of light on the human condition that would entitle us to rebrand ourselves as neurophilosophers.

---

[3] Jerry A. Fodor, *The Modularity of Mind: An Essay in Faculty Psychology* (Cambridge, MA: MIT Press, 1983).

Overdetermination

Consider the evolutionary psychologist's explanation of altruism as we find it delicately and passionately expounded by Matt Ridley in his book *The Origins of Virtue*.[4] Ridley plausibly suggests that moral virtue and the habit of obedience to what Kant called the moral law is an adaptation, his evidence being that any other form of conduct would have set an organism's genes at a distinct disadvantage in the game of life. To use the language of game theory, in the circumstances that have prevailed during the course of evolution, altruism is a dominant strategy. This was shown by John Maynard Smith in a paper first published in 1964, and taken up by Robert Axelrod in his famous book *The Evolution of Cooperation*, which appeared in 1984.[5] But what exactly do those writers mean by "altruism"?

An organism acts altruistically, they tell us, if it benefits another organism at a cost to itself. The concept applies equally to the soldier ant that marches into the flames that threaten the anthill, and to the officer who throws himself onto the live grenade that threatens his platoon. The concept of altruism, so understood, cannot explain, or even recognize, the distinction between those two cases. Yet surely there is all the difference in the world between the ant that marches instinctively toward the flames, unable either to understand what it is doing or to fear the results of it, and the officer who consciously lays down his life for his troops.

If Kant is right, a rational being has a motive to obey the moral law, regardless of genetic advantage. This motive would arise, even if the normal result of following it were that which the Greeks observed with awe at Thermopylae, or the Anglo-Saxons at the Battle of Maldon. In such instances an entire community is observed to embrace death, in full consciousness of what it is doing, because death is the honorable option. Even if you don't think Kant's account of this is the right one, the fact is that this motive is universally observed in human beings, and is entirely distinct from that of the soldier ant, in

[4]Ridley, *The Origins of Virtue*.

[5]Smith, "Group Selection and Kin Selection," and John Maynard Smith and G. R. Price, "The Logic of Animal Conflict," *Nature* 246 (1973): 15–18; Robert Axelrod, *The Evolution of Cooperation* (New York: Basic Books, 1984).

being founded on a consciousness of the predicament, of the cost of doing right, and of the call to renounce life for the sake of others who depend on you or to whom your life is owed.

To put it in another way, on the approach of the evolutionary psychologists, the conduct of the Spartans at Thermopylae is overdetermined. The "dominant reproductive strategy" explanation, and the "honorable sacrifice" explanation are both sufficient to account for this conduct. So which is the real explanation? Or is the "honorable sacrifice" explanation just a story that we tell ourselves, in order to pin medals on the chest of the ruined "survival machine" that died in obedience to its genes?

But suppose that the moral explanation is genuine and sufficient. It would follow that the genetic explanation is trivial. If rational beings are motivated to behave in this way, regardless of any genetic strategy, then that is sufficient to explain the fact that they do behave in this way. And being disposed to behave in this way is an adaptation—for all this means is that people who were disposed by nature to behave in any other way would by now have died out, regardless of the reasons they might have had for behaving as they did.

This brings us again to the parallel with mathematics that I discussed in the first chapter. We can easily show that mathematical competence is an adaptation. But that says nothing about the distinction between valid and invalid proofs, and it won't give us a grasp of mathematical reasoning. There is an *internal* discipline involved here, which will not be illuminated by any amount of psychology, just as there is an internal discipline of moral thinking, which leads of its own accord to the conclusion that a given action is obligatory.[6] Of course, it is a further fact about human beings that they are disposed to do what they think they ought to do. But it is the moral judgment, rather than some blind instinct, that compels them. The parallel is not exact. But it illustrates the way in which evolutionary explanations reduce to triviality, when the thing to be explained contains its own principles of persuasion.

Moreover, like mathematics, moral thinking unfolds before us a view of the world that transcends the deliverances of the senses, and

[6]See again O'Hear, *Beyond Evolution*.

which it is hard to explain as the by-product of evolutionary competition. Moral judgments are framed in the language of necessity, and no corner of our universe escapes their jurisdiction. Morality provides another example of the way in which intentionality "reaches beyond" the order of nature, relating us in thought to the cosmos as a whole. And morality makes sense only if there are reasons for action that are normative and binding. It is hard to accept this, and still to resist the conclusion drawn by Thomas Nagel, that the universe is ordered by teleological laws.[7]

The Idea of Information

Cognitive science concerns the way in which information is processed by truth-directed creatures. And it aims to explain perception, belief, and decision in terms of the information-processing functions that they encapsulate. However, is there a single notion of information at work here? When I inform you of something, I also inform you *that* something: I say, for example, that the plane carrying your wife has landed. Information, in this sense, is an intentional concept, which describes states that can be identified only through their content. Intentionality, the focusing on representations, is a well-known obstacle in the way of all stimulus-response accounts of cognitive states; but why is it not an obstacle in the way of cognitive science?

It is surely obvious that the concept of information as information *that* is not the concept that has evolved in computer science, or in the cybernetic models of human mental processes. In these models information means the accumulated instructions for taking this or that exit from a binary pathway. Information is delivered by algorithms, relating inputs to outputs within a digital system. These algorithms express no opinions; they do not commit the computer to living up to them or incorporating them into its decisions, for it doesn't make decisions or have opinions.

What I mean can be clarified by an example. Suppose a computer is programmed to "read," as we say, a digitally encoded input, which it

[7] See again *Mind and Cosmos*.

translates into pixels, causing it to display the picture of a woman on its screen. In order to describe this process, we do not need to refer to the woman in the picture. The entire process can be completely described in terms of the hardware that translates digital data into pixels, and the software, or algorithm, which contains the instructions for doing this. There is neither the need nor the right, in this case, to use concepts like those of seeing, thinking, observing, in describing what the computer is doing; nor do we have either the need or the right to describe the thing observed in the picture as playing any causal role, or any role at all, in the operation of the computer. Of course, *we* see the woman in the picture. And to us the picture contains information of quite another kind from that encoded in the digitalized instructions for producing it. It conveys information about a woman and how she looks. To describe this kind of information is impossible without the use of intentional language—language that describes the content of certain thoughts rather than the object to which those thoughts refer.

Consider Botticelli's famous painting *The Birth of Venus* (fig. 1). You are well aware that there is no such scene in reality as the one depicted, that there is no such goddess as Venus, and that this indelible image is an image of nothing real. But there she is all the same. Actually there was a real woman who served as Botticelli's model—Simonetta Vespucci, mistress of Lorenzo de' Medici. But the painting is not *of* or *about* Simonetta. In looking at this picture you are looking at a fiction, and that is something you know, and something that conditions any interpretation you might offer of its meaning. This is the goddess of erotic love—but in Plato's version of the erotic, according to which desire calls us away from the world of sensual attachments to the ideal form of the beautiful (which is, incidentally, what Simonetta was for Botticelli). This painting helps to make Plato's theory both clear and believable—it is a work of concentrated thought that changes, or ought to change, the worldview of anyone who looks at it for long. There is a world of information contained in this image—but it is information *about* something, information *that*, which is not captured by the algorithm that a computer might use to translate it, pixel for pixel, onto the screen.

The question is how do we move from the one concept of information to the other? How do we explain the emergence of thoughts *about* something from processes that are entirely explained by the

Fig. 1. Sandro Botticelli, *The Birth of Venus*, Florence, Galleria degli Uffizi. © 2013. Photo SCALA, Florence—courtesy of the Ministero Beni e Att. Culturali.

transformation of visually encoded data? Cognitive science doesn't tell us. And computer models of the brain won't tell us either. They might show how images get encoded in digitalized format and transmitted in that format by neural pathways to the center where they are "interpreted." But that center does not in fact *interpret*—interpreting is a process that *we* do, in drawing conclusions, retrieving information *that*, and seeing what is there before us. And also what is *not* there, like the goddess Venus in Botticelli's picture. A skeptic about intentionality might say that this simply shows that, in the last analysis, there is only *one* scientifically respectable concept of information— that there is, in reality, no such thing as *aboutness*, and therefore no question as to how we proceed from one concept of information to the other.[8] But we would need a strong independent argument before drawing this conclusion. After all, isn't science *about* the world, and

---

[8]This paradoxical position is defended by Alex Rosenberg in *The Atheist's Guide to Reality: Enjoying Life without Illusions* (New York: W. W. Norton and Co., 2011); well may you ask what his book is about.

does it not consist precisely in information of the kind that the skeptic denies to exist?

The Mereological Fallacy

In their controversial book, *The Philosophical Foundations of Neuroscience*, Max Bennett and Peter Hacker describe something that they call the "mereological fallacy," from *meros*, a part, and "mereology," the branch of logic that studies the part/whole relation.[9] This is the fallacy, as they suppose it to be, of explaining some feature of a thing by ascribing that *very same feature* to a part of the thing. One familiar case of this is the well-known homunculus fallacy in the philosophy of mind, sometimes associated with Descartes, who tried to explain the consciousness of a human being by the presence of an inner soul, the "real me" inside. And clearly, that was no explanation, but merely a transferral of the problem.

Bennett and Hacker believe that many cognitive scientists commit this fallacy, when they write of the brain "forming images," "interpreting data," being conscious or aware of things, making choices, and so on. And it certainly would be a fallacy to think that you could explain something like consciousness in this way, by showing how the brain is conscious of this or that—the explanation would be self-evidently circular.

Dennett and others object that no cognitive scientist ever intended to produce explanations of that kind.[10] For Dennett there is no reason why we should not use intentional idioms to describe the behavior of entities that are not persons, and not conscious—just as we can use them, he believes, to describe simple feedback mechanisms like thermostats. When the thermostat acts to switch on the cooling system, because the room has reached a certain temperature, it is responding to information from the outside world. Sometimes it makes mistakes

---

[9] Max Bennett and Peter Hacker, *The Philosophical Foundations of Neuroscience* (Oxford: Blackwell, 2003). On mereology, see the illuminating study by Peter Simons, *Parts: A Study in Ontology* (Oxford: Oxford University Press, 1987).

[10] See Daniel C. Dennett, in *Neuroscience and Philosophy: Brain, Mind, and Language*, ed. Dan Robinson (New York: Columbia University Press, 2007).

and heats the room instead of cooling it. You can "trick" it by blowing hot air over it. And in more complex devices like a computer it becomes yet more obvious that the mental language we apply to each other provides a useful way of describing, predicting, and making general sense of what computers do. In Dennett's view there is nothing anthropomorphic in my reference to what my computer thinks, what it wants me to do next, and so on. As I remarked in the previous chapter, for Dennett I am simply taking up what he calls the "intentional stance" toward something that thereby yields to my attempts to explain it. Its behavior can be successfully predicted using intentional idioms. Likewise with the brain: I can apply intentional idioms to a brain or its parts, without thereby implying the existence of another conscious individual—other, that is, than the person whose brain this is. And in doing this I might in fact be explaining the connections between input and output that we observe in the complete human organism, and in that sense be giving a theory of consciousness.

There is an element of justice in Dennett's riposte. There is no reason to suppose, when we use intentional idioms in describing brain processes and cognitive systems generally, that we are thereby committing ourselves to a homunculus-like *center* of consciousness, which is being described exactly as a person might be described in attributing thought, feeling, or intention. The problem, however, is that we know how to eliminate the intentional idioms from our description of the thermostat. We can also eliminate them, with a little more difficulty, from our description of the computer. But the cognitive-science descriptions of the digital brain seem to take us to the point required— the point of explaining *consciousness*—only if we retain the intentional idioms, and refuse to replace them. Suppose one day we can give a complete account of the brain in terms of the processing of digitalized information between input and output. We can then relinquish the intentional stance when describing the workings of this thing, just as we can with the thermostat. But we will not, then, be describing the consciousness of a person. We will be describing something that goes on when people think, and which is necessary to their thinking. But we won't be describing their thought, any more than we will be describing either the birth of Venus or Plato's theory of erotic love when we specify all the pixels in a screened version of Botticelli's painting.

Some philosophers—notably Searle—have argued that the brain is the seat of consciousness, and that there is no a priori obstacle to discovering the neural networks in which, as Searle puts it, consciousness is "realized." This seems to me to be a fudge. I don't exactly know what is intended by the term "realized": could consciousness be realized in neural pathways in one kind of thing, in silicon chips in another, and in strings and levers in another? Or is it necessarily connected with networks that deliver a particular kind of connection between input and output? If so, what kind? The kind that we witness in animals and people, when we describe them as conscious? In that case, we have not advanced from the position that consciousness is a property of the whole animal, and the whole person, and not of any particular part of it.

All of that is intricate, and pursuing it will lead into territory that has been worked over again and again by recent philosophers, to the point of becoming, in my view, utterly sterile.

The First-Person Case

Besides, I don't think that the real problem for cognitive science is the problem of consciousness. Indeed, I am not sure that it is even a problem. Consciousness is a feature that we share with the higher animals, and I see it as an "emergent" feature, which is in place just as soon as behavior and the functional relations that govern it reach a certain level of complexity.[11] The real problem, as I see it, is self-consciousness—the first-person awareness that distinguishes us from the other animals, and which enables us to identify ourselves, and to attribute mental predicates to ourselves, in the first-person case—the very same predicates that others attribute to us in the second- and third-person case.

Some people think we can make sense of this if we can identify a *self*, an inner monitor, which records the mental states that occur within its field of awareness, and marks them up, so to speak, on an

---

[11] To put it another way: consciousness is part of the *life* of the higher animals. See Alva Noë, *Out of Our Heads* (New York: Hill and Wang, 2009).

inner screen. Sometimes it looks to me as though Antonio Damasio is arguing in this way:[12] but of course it exposes him immediately to Bennett and Hacker's argument, and again duplicates the problem that it is meant to solve. How does the monitor find out about the mental goings-on within its field of view? Could it make mistakes? Could it make a misattribution of a mental state, picking out the wrong subject of consciousness? Some people have argued that this is what goes on in the phenomenon of "inserted thought," which characterizes certain forms of mental illness. But there is no reason to think that a person who receives such "inserted thoughts" could ever be mistaken in thinking that they are going on in *him*.[13]

The monitor theory is an attempt to read self-consciousness into the mechanism that supposedly explains it. We are familiar with a puzzling feature of persons, namely, that, through mastering the first-person use of mental predicates, they are able to make certain statements about themselves with a kind of epistemological privilege. People are immune not only to "error through misidentification," as Shoemaker puts it, but also (in the case of certain mental states like pain) to "error through misascription."[14] It is one of the deep truths about our condition, that we enjoy these first-person immunities. If we did not do so, we could not in fact enter into dialogue with each other: we would be always describing ourselves as though we were someone else. However, first-person privilege is a feature of people, construed as language-using creatures: it is a condition connected in some way with their mastery of self-reference and self-predication. Internal monitors, whether situated in the brain or elsewhere, are not "language-using creatures": they do not enter into their competence through participating in the linguistic network. Hence they cannot possibly have competences that derive from language use and which are enshrined in and dependent upon the deep grammar of self-reference.

[12] See, for example, Antonio Damasio, *Looking for Spinoza: Joy, Sorrow, and the Feeling Brain* (New York: Harcourt, 2003).

[13] For a useful summary of this issue, see George Graham, "Self-Ascription" in *The Philosophy of Psychiatry: A Companion*, ed. Jennifer Radden (Oxford: Oxford University Press, 2004).

[14] Sidney Shoemaker, *Self-Knowledge and Self-Identity* (Ithaca, NY: Cornell University Press, 1963).

This is not to deny that there is, at some level, a neurological explanation of self-knowledge. There must be, just as there must be a neurological explanation of any other mental capacity that is revealed in behavior—although not necessarily a *complete* explanation, since the nervous system is, after all, only one part of the human being, who is himself incomplete as a person until brought into developing relation with the surrounding world and with others of his kind (for, as I shall go on to argue, personhood is a relational feature). But this explanation will not be framed in terms taken directly from the language of mind. It will not be describing persons at all, but ganglia and neurons, digitally organized synapses and processes that are only figuratively described by the use of mental language in just the way my computer is only figuratively described when I refer to it as unhappy or angry. There is no doubt a neurological cause of "inserted thoughts." But it will not be framed in terms of thoughts in the brain that are in some way wrongly connected up by the inner monitor. There is probably no way in which we can, by peering hard, so to speak, at the phenomenology of inserted thoughts, make a guess at the neural disorder that gives rise to them.

Words like "I," "choose," "responsible," and so on have no part in neurological science, which can explain why an organism utters those words, but can give no material content to them. Indeed, one of the recurrent mistakes in neuroscience is the mistake of looking for the referents of such words—seeking the place in the brain where the "self" resides, or the material correlate of human freedom. The excitement over mirror neurons has its origins here—in the belief that we have found the neural basis of the self concept and of our ability to see others too as selves.[15] But all such ideas disappear from the science of human behavior, once we see human behavior as the product of a digitally organized nervous system.

On the other hand, ideas of the self and freedom cannot disappear from the minds of the human subjects themselves. Their behavior

---

[15]The discovery of mirror neurons (which fire both when subjects perform an action and when they observe another perform it) is due to Giacomo Rizzolatti. The extravagant speculations to which the discovery has given rise are well illustrated by V. S. Ramachandran's article on the topic, "Mirror Neurons and Imitation Learning," available on Edge, http://edge.org/conversation/mirror-neurons-and-imitation-learning-as-the-driving-force-behind-the-great-leap-forward-in-human-evolution.

toward each other is mediated by the belief in freedom, in selfhood, in the knowledge that I am I and you are you and that each of us is a center of free and responsible thought and action. Out of these beliefs arises the world of interpersonal responses, and it is from the relations established between us that our own self-conception derives. It would seem to follow that we need to clarify the concepts of the self, of free choice, of responsibility and the rest, if we are to have a clear conception of what we are, and that no amount of neuroscience is going to help us in this task. We live on the surface, and what matters to us are not the invisible nervous systems that explain how people work, but the visible appearances to which we respond when we respond to them as people. It is these appearances that we interpret, and upon our interpretation we build responses that must in turn be interpreted by those to whom they are directed.

Again we have a useful parallel in the study of pictures. There is no way in which we could, by peering hard at the face in Botticelli's Venus, recuperate a chemical breakdown of the pigments used to compose it. Of course, if we peer hard at the canvas and the substances smeared on it, we can reach an understanding of its chemistry. But then we are not peering at the face—not even *seeing* it.

I think we can understand the problem more clearly if we ask ourselves what would happen if we had a *complete* brain science, one that enabled us to fulfill Churchland's dream, and replace folk psychology with the supposedly true theory of the mind. What happens then to first-person awareness? In order to know that I am in a certain state, would I have to submit to a brain scan? Surely, if the *true* theory of the mind is a theory of what goes on in the neural pathways, I would have to find out about my own mental states as I find out about yours, achieving certainty only when I have tracked them down to their neural essence. My best observations would be of the form "It seems as though such-and-such is going on . . ." But then the first-person case has vanished, and only the third-person case remains. Or has it? If we look a little closer, we see that in fact the "I" remains in this picture. For the expression "It seems as though," in the report that I just imagined, in fact means "It seems to me as though," which means "I am having an experience of this kind," and to that statement first-person privilege attaches. It does not report something that I have to find out, or which could be mistaken. So what *does* it report?

Somehow the "I" is still there, on the edge of things, and the neuro-science has merely shifted that edge. The conscious state is not that which is being described in terms of activity in the nervous system, but that which is being *expressed* in the statement "It seems to me as though . . ."

Moreover, I could not eliminate this "I," this first-person viewpoint, and still retain the things on which human life and community have been built. As I argued in the previous chapter, the I-You relation is fundamental to the human condition. We are accountable to each other, and this accountability depends on our ability to give and take reasons, which in turn depends upon first-person awareness. But the concepts involved in this process—concepts of responsibility, inten-tion, guilt, and so on—have no place in brain science. They bring with them a rival conceptual scheme, which is, I should like to say, in inevitable tension with *any* biological science of the human condition.

Cognitive Dualism Yet Again

So how should a philosopher approach the findings of neuroscience? I don't want to say that I am something *other* than this organism that stands before you. This here thing is what I am. The best way of proceeding, it seems to me, is through the kind of cognitive dualism I adumbrated earlier, whereby we can grasp the idea that there can be *one* reality, which is understood in more than one way. In describ-ing a sequence of sounds as a melody, I am situating the sequence in the human world: the world of our responses, intentions, and self-knowledge. I am lifting the sounds out of the physical realm, and repositioning them in the *Lebenswelt*, which is a world of freedom, reason, and interpersonal being. But I am not describing something *other* than the sounds, or implying that there is something hiding behind the sounds, some inner "self" or essence that reveals itself to itself in some way inaccessible to me. I am describing what I hear *in* the sounds, when I respond to them as music. In something like that way I situate the human organism in the *Lebenswelt*; and in doing so I use another language, and with other intentions, than those that apply in the biological sciences.

The analogy is imperfect, of course, like all analogies, though I shall return to it later, when discussing the problem of musical meaning. But it points to the way out of the neuroscientist's dilemma. Instead of taking the high road of theory that Patricia Churchland recommends, attempting to provide a neurological account of what we mean when we talk of persons and their states of mind, we should take the low road of common sense, and recognize that neuroscience describes one *aspect* of people, in language that cannot capture what we mean, when we describe what we are thinking, feeling, or intending. Personhood is an "emergent" feature of the human being in the way that music is an emergent feature of sounds: not something over and above the life and behavior in which we observe it, but not reducible to them either. Once personhood has emerged, it is possible to relate to an organism in a new way—the way of personal relations. (In like manner we can relate to music in ways in which we cannot relate to something that we hear merely as a sequence of sounds—for example, we can dance to it.) With this new order of relation comes a new order of understanding, in which reasons and meanings, rather than causes, are sought in answer to the question "why?" With persons we are in dialogue: we call upon them to justify their conduct in our eyes, as we must justify our conduct in theirs. Central to this dialogue is the feature of self-awareness. This does not mean that people are really "selves" that hide within their bodies. It means that their *own way of describing* themselves is privileged, and cannot be dismissed as mere "folk psychology," which will give way in time to a proper neuroscience.

This point has great bearing on the argument of the previous chapter. As I argued there, cognitive dualism makes sense so long as "ontological priority" is accorded to the scientific worldview. The *Lebenswelt* stands to the order of nature in a relation of emergence. But this relation is not reducible to a one-to-one relation between particulars. We cannot say of any individual identified in one way that it is the *same individual* as one identified in the other way. We cannot say "one thing, two conceptions," since that raises the question what thing, which raises the question, under which conception is the thing identified? Spinoza saw this point, and therefore removed the "thing" concept entirely from his ontology, and reshaped the concept of substance as a name for the whole of the world. There are no "individual substances" in Spinoza's conception of reality.

You can see the problem very clearly in the case of persons, since here, if I say one thing, two conceptions, and then ask *what* thing, the answer will depend upon which "cognitive scheme" I am "within" at the time. The answer could be: this animal; or it could be: this person. And we know these are different answers, from all the literature on the problem of personal identity. In other words each scheme provides its own way of dividing up the world, and the schemes are incommensurable. Because the concept of personhood is so difficult, we are tempted to duck out of the problem, and say that there is just *one* way of identifying what we are talking about, using the concept "human being" to cross back and forth from scientific to interpersonal ways of seeing things—which is what David Wiggins does in *Sameness and Substance*, for example, and Peter Hacker in his Wittgensteinian defense of our everyday conceptual apparatus.[16] But seeing things in that way, it seems to me, we underplay the difference that is made by the first-person case. My self-awareness enables me to identify myself without reference to my physical coordinates. I am assured of my identity through time without consulting the spatiotemporal history of my body—and this fact gives a peculiar metaphysical resonance to the question "where in the world am I?"

Light is cast on this issue by Aristotle's hylomorphism. Aristotle believed that the relation between body and soul is one of matter and form—the soul being the organizing principle, the body the matter from which the human being is composed. The suggestion is obscure and the analogies given by Aristotle are unpersuasive. But the theory becomes clearer when expressed in terms of the relation between a whole and its parts. Thus Mark Johnston has defended, in the name of hylomorphism, the view that the essential nature of an individual thing is given by the concept under which its parts are gathered together in a unity.[17] If we accept that approach, then we should, I think, conclude that in the case of human beings there

[16]David Wiggins, *Sameness and Substance Renewed* (Cambridge: Cambridge University Press, 2007); P.M.S. Hacker *Insight and Illusion* (Oxford: Oxford University Press, 1972), new ed. 1986—but see Hacker's website.

[17]See Mark Johnston, "Hylomorphism," *Journal of Philosophy* 103, no. 12 (2006): 652–98.

are two such unifying concepts—that of the human organism, and that of the person, each embedded within a conceptual scheme that sets out to explain or to understand its subject matter. In this way cognitive dualism casts a kind of ontological shadow. Humans are organized from their material constituents in two distinct and incommensurable ways—as animal and as person. Each human being is indeed two things, but not two separable things, since those two things reside in the same place at the same time, and all the parts of the one are also parts of the other. Hence a kind of ontological dualism arises, as a by-product of cognitive dualism. It does not force us to believe in a realm of mysterious entities hiding within the interstices, so to speak, of the physical world. It is simply a shadow cast across the order of nature by the light of our mutual dealings.

But this raises a skeptical question. Granted that we see each other as persons, and that, in doing so, we organize the human material in a way distinct from any natural science, what guarantee do we have that we are not dealing in fictions? Might the concepts of person, freedom, reason, and accountability form a shared hallucination, a *délibáb*, as the Hungarians say, which will vanish when the matter of human life is seen as it should be seen, with the cool eye of science? Indeed, by admitting the ontological priority of the "scientific image," have I not already opened the way to that riposte? The rest of this book will be a sustained reply to that skeptical question. And the reply begins, as it must, from the problem of free will.

Subject and Object

In a well-known series of experiments Benjamin Libet has used brain-imaging techniques to explore the causal antecedents of human choice.[18] His results show that when people choose between alternative movements, there is a particular burst of activity in the motor centers of the brain leading directly to the action. But the subjects themselves report their decision always some moments after this,

[18]The best source here is Libet's contribution to *The Oxford Handbook of Free Will*, ed. Robert Kane, 2nd ed. (Oxford: Oxford University Press, 2011).

when the action is already (from the point of view of the central nervous system) "under way." The conclusion often drawn from these experiments is that the "brain" decides what to do, and our consciousness follows only later, when the switch has already been flipped. But that conclusion in no way follows from the data. Sometimes an intentional action is preceded by a decision or choice, certainly; but usually the action *is* the choice. And what makes it intentional is not that it arose in a particular way, but that the subject can say on no basis that *I* did this, or am doing this, and in doing so make himself accountable for it. To say that we are free is to point to this fact: namely, that we can justify and criticize our actions, lay claim to them as our own, and know immediately and with certainty what we will do—not by predicting what we will do but by deciding to do it. (Hence Anscombe's idea that intentional action is distinguished by the application of a "certain sense of the question 'why?'".)[19] Freedom emerges from the web of interpersonal relations, and comes into being as a corollary of "I," "you," and "why?"

You might say of Libet's experiments that they attempt to discover the place of the subject in the world of objects. They are looking for the point of intersection of the free self-consciousness with the world in which it acts. And they do not find that point. All that they find is a succession of events in the stream of objects, none of which can be identified with a free self-conscious choice. There is a parallel here with the question that I raised in the first chapter: the question of God's presence in the world. If you look on the world with the eyes of science, it is impossible to find the place, the time, or the particular sequence of events that can be interpreted as showing God's presence. God disappears from the world, as soon as we address it with the "why?" of explanation, just as human persons disappear from the world, when we look for the neurological explanation of their acts. For God, if he exists, is a person like us, whose identity and will are bound up with his nature as a subject. Maybe we shall find him in the world where we are only if we cease to invoke him with the "why?" of cause, and conjure him with the "why?" of reason instead. And the "why?" of reason is addressed from I to you. The God of

[19] See Anscombe, *Intention*.

the philosophers disappeared behind the world, because he was described in the third person, and not addressed in the second.

There is a connection here with the Christian theology of the Incarnation. In Phil. 2:7 Saint Paul describes Christ as having "emptied himself" (ἑαυτον εκενωσεν) and taken the form of a slave, so as "to become obedient unto death." This passage is authority for the view that God can be present among us only by a self-emptying (*kenosis*) in which the divine attributes are in some way left to one side, made inoperative by a sacrificial posture of which God alone is fully capable. Simone Weil adds that God can show himself in this world only by entirely withdrawing from it: to appear among us clothed in the divine attributes would be to absorb and annihilate what is *not* God, and so to undo the work of creation.[20] To love God is to love an absence, and this absence is made present to us in Christ, the person whose being is also a self-abnegation. Weil's thought is of course mysterious, verging on the self-contradictory. But the believer will say that this should not surprise us, for we are here at the edge of the natural order, exploring the horizon of our world. We cannot confront the creator in a direct I-to-You encounter, since this would lead to our annihilation: "thou canst not see my face, for there shall no man see me and live" (Exod. 33:20). But in his self-emptying in Christ, God shows his freedom and makes it possible for us to address him as a Thou. This self-emptying is rehearsed in the Eucharist, the act of communion that is performed "in remembrance of me"—in other words, in recognition of God's presence among us as an I.

Overreaching Intentionality

I shall later return to those mystical thoughts. Meanwhile, however, it is necessary to address the topic of self-consciousness, in order to lay the foundations for my ensuing argument. Many philosophers have referred to the "mystery" of consciousness, as though consciousness were a peculiar feature of the world that cannot be reconciled with the ordinary assumptions of physics. But this is deeply

[20] Simone Weil, *Gravity and Grace* (London: Routledge and Kegan Paul, 1952).

misleading. If there is a mystery here, it does not lie in some peculiar stuff, or fact, or realm in the world of objects. The mystery, such as it is, arises from the privileged view of the subject, and lies on the horizon within which the world of the subject plays itself out. No attempt to pin down the subject in the world of objects will ever really succeed. You can extract from the person as many body parts as you will, but you will never find the place where he is, the place from which he addresses me and which I in turn address. What matters to us are not the invisible nervous systems that explain how people work, but the visible appearances to which we respond when we respond to them as people. It is these appearances that we interpret, and upon our interpretation we build responses that must in turn be interpreted by those to whom they are directed. These responses are directed not to some item in the world that we share, but to the horizon, the I, that identifies the other's point of view, and which only the other can occupy. It seems then that there is an impassable metaphysical gap, between the human object, and the free subject to whom we relate as a person. Yet we constantly cross that gap. How is this?

All philosophical inquiry, Kant argued, begins and ends in the point of view of the subject. If I ask myself what I can know, or what I must do, or what I may hope for, then the question is about what *I* can know, and so on, given the limitations of my perspective. It is not a question about what God can know, what is knowable from some point of view that I could never attain to, or what is knowable from no point of view at all. To answer the question, therefore, I must first understand my own perspective—which means understanding what must be true of me, if I am to ask the philosophical question.

I know that I am a single and unified subject of experience. This present thought, this pain, this hope, and this memory are features of *one* thing, and that thing is what I am. I know this on no basis, without having to carry out any kind of check, and, indeed, without the use of criteria of any kind—this is what is (or what ought to be) meant by the term "transcendental." The unity of the self-conscious subject is not the conclusion of any inquiry, but the presupposition of all inquiries. The unity of consciousness "transcends" all argument since it is the premise without which argument makes no sense.

This "transcendental unity of apperception" contains also a claim to identity through time. I attribute to myself states of mind—memories, hopes, intentions, and so on—which reach into the past and the future, and which represent me as enduring through time. How is this possible, and with what warrant do I affirm my self-identity as an objective truth about the world? Those questions underlie the argument of Kant's "transcendental deduction of the categories," and this is not the place to discuss them. More important is Kant's expanded version of the transcendental subject, as he develops this in his ethical theory and also (although this is not often noticed) in his aesthetics.

The fundamental question of practical reason is addressed to *me*, and it asks, "what shall *I* do?" I can answer this question only on the assumption that I am free. This assumption has a transcendental ground, since it is the premise of all practical reasoning and never the conclusion of it. Transcendental freedom, like the transcendental unity of apperception, belongs to my perspective on the world. It is not a perspective that could be adopted by an animal, since it depends upon the use of the word "I"—the ability to identify myself in the first person, and to give and accept reasons for believing what I believe, doing what I do, and feeling what I feel.

Fichte and Hegel developed those thoughts to provide a new form of insight into the human condition. The immediate awareness that characterizes the position of the subject is, Hegel argued, abstract and indeterminate. It involves no concrete determination of *what* is known or intended by the subject. If we were pure subjects, existing in a metaphysical void, as Descartes imagined, we should never advance to the point of knowledge, not even knowledge of ourselves, nor should we be able to aim at a determinate goal. Our awareness would remain abstract and empty, an awareness of nothing determinate or concrete. But as transcendental subject, I do not merely stand at the edge of my world. I encounter others within that world. I am I to myself only because, and to the extent that, I am you to another. I must therefore be capable of the free dialogue in which I take charge of my presence before the presence of you. That is what it means, to understand the first-person case. And it is because I understand the first-person case that I have immediate awareness of my condition. The position that, for Kant, defines the premise of philosophy and, which is presupposed in every argument, itself rests on a presupposition—the presupposition of the other, the one against whom I try myself in contest and in dialogue. "I" requires "you," and the two meet in the world of objects.

The suggestion is illustrated by Hegel with a series of parables, concerning the "realization" of the subject—its *Entäusserung*, or objectification—in the world of objects. Some of these parables (I am reluctant to call them arguments) are discussed in the literature of political science, notably that of the master and slave. Many of them convey profound truths about the human condition, and about the social nature of the self. However, the idealist metaphysics to which Hegel's narrative supposedly leads—the metaphysics of the "absolute idea"—is, it seems to me, neither defensible nor fully intelligible. The lasting sense of what Hegel means can be grasped, I believe, only if we adhere closely to the concept from which the narrative begins, which is the concept of the subject, as the defining feature of the human condition, and the feature to which the mystery of the world is owed.

Contained in this concept is what I call the "overreaching intentionality of interpersonal attitudes." In all our responses to each other, whether love or hate, affection or disaffection, approval or disapproval, anger or desire, we look *into* the other, in search of that unattainable horizon from which he or she addresses us. We are animals swimming in the currents of causality, who relate to each other in space and time. But in the I-to-You encounter we do not see each other in that way. Each human object is also a subject, addressing us in looks, gestures, and words, from the transcendental horizon of the "I." Our responses to others aim toward that horizon, passing on beyond the body to the being that it incarnates. It is this feature of our interpersonal responses that gives such compelling force to the myth of the soul, of the true but hidden self that is veiled by the flesh. And because of this our interpersonal responses develop in a certain way: we see each other as wrapped within those responses, so to speak, and we hold each other to account for them as though they originated ex nihilo from the unified center of the self. You may say that, when we see each other in this way, we are giving credence to a metaphysical doctrine, maybe even a metaphysical myth. But it is not Descartes's doctrine of the soul-substance, nor is it obviously a myth. Moreover, a doctrine that is enshrined in our basic personal emotions, which cannot be eliminated without undermining the I-You relationship on which our first-person understanding depends, cannot be dismissed as a simple error. It has something of the status that Kant attributes to the original unity of consciousness—the status of a presupposition of our thinking, including the thinking that might lead us to cast doubt on it. Indeed, on one understanding of the matter, the adherence to this presupposition, and the practice that flows from it, is what Kant's transcendental freedom really amounts to.

The indispensable presence in our lives of this overreaching intentionality is at the root of philosophy, and is the real reason that people find evolutionary and reductionist perspectives on the human condition so hard to accept. It also explains the oft-heard complaint that, while our secular societies make room for morality, for knowledge, and for the life of the mind, they suffer from a spiritual deficit. Human beings, we hear, have a "spiritual" dimension, with spiritual needs and values, and people say such things even though they withhold assent from any religion, and even though they reject the old myth of the soul, or regard it as an elaborate metaphor. The reason, I believe, is this: the "overreaching intentionality" of our interpersonal attitudes is not an unalterable given; it can be educated, turned in new directions, disciplined through virtues, and corrupted through vice. In some cases of extreme autism it may even be lacking, as it is lacking in animals. But learning to direct your attitudes to the horizon of the other's being, from which he in turn directs his gaze— this requires a discipline that goes further than mere respect. In all that touches what is deepest and most lasting in our lives—religious faith, erotic love, friendship, family ties, and the enjoyment of art, music, and literature—we address the horizon from which the other's gaze is seeking us. Moral education involves the maintenance of this overreaching intentionality, so as to make it possible, in the hardest circumstances, to look the other person in the I. That is what people mean by "spiritual" discipline, and it is what Plato called "the care of the soul." It is vanishing from our world today, for reasons that I do not need to elaborate. But in what follows I will try to show why this matters.

4

....

The First-Person Plural

In the previous chapter I gave reasons for thinking that our self-understanding as persons cannot be replaced by any natural science of the human being. I did not deny that we are animals, or that our behavior and mental life are largely governed by the computational processes that occur in our brains. But, I suggested, we know ourselves, and each other, under a concept that denotes no natural kind and which takes its sense from the network of our free interactions: the concept of the person, itself to be explained in terms of first-person knowledge and the I-to-You encounter. One consequence of this is that we could not replace our way of understanding each other with some science, however comprehensive, of the human brain. The human world, ordered by first-person awareness, emerges from the order of nature, while remaining incommensurable with it.

First-person awareness and practical reason (the giving and taking of reasons for action) are the forces that shape the human person. These forces, I maintain, are unaffected by the proof that our actions, thoughts, and perceptions are dependent on a vast machinery of brain processes of which we are not aware. As I argued in the previous chapter, we are tempted to construe the I-You encounter as an encounter between objects that exist in some other dimension from the physical world around them. But, to repeat, I am arguing that there is a cognitive dualism underlying our response to the human world, and that any ontological dualism (for example, the dualism of human animal and human person) must be understood as a shadow cast across the order of nature by our twofold way of understanding things. Whether this twofold way of understanding is sustained by teleological laws is a question that we are not yet equipped to address. Suffice it to say that we can describe and understand first-person knowledge without any recourse to a mysterious "inner" realm of the kind postulated by Descartes. And we can do this, even while recognizing that the division between subject and object is absolute and irreducible.

The I-You encounter is an encounter between subjects, and one that can be understood only if we recognize that the logic of first-person awareness is built into the concepts through which our mutual dealings are shaped. And those concepts in turn shape the *Lebenswelt*, which is a world of appearances, made present to us in experience. Unlike the order of nature the *Lebenswelt* has no hidden or purely postulated parts. It is understood through concepts of functional, moral, and aesthetic kinds, through the interests that unite and divide us, and in terms that are open at every point to the ideas of "I," "you," and "why?" as these are deployed in our mutual dialogue. It is a world that contains melodies as well as sounds, faces as well as physiognomies, meanings as well as causes. And all these are real and objective features of it, even if they are never mentioned in the book of empirical science.

Taking inspiration from the work of J. L. Austin, John Searle has emphasized what he calls "declarations"—the speech acts, such as naming and promising, that bring into being the situations to which they refer. When I promise to visit you tomorrow, I create an obligation to visit, which henceforth exists as an institutional fact—a fact about the realm of human relations.[1] Likewise when a legislature passes a law, the declaration of the law creates the law that it describes, which exists henceforth as an obligation weighing on all members of the relevant community. Searle's suggestion provides a useful starting point for my argument in this chapter. It reminds us that people are able to relate to each other not merely by indicating their desires, as animals do, but by undertaking obligations, making promises, committing themselves, and in general taking responsibility for the future and for the well-being of others. And in doing

---

[1] Searle has argued, in "How to Derive 'Ought' from 'Is,'" *Philosophical Review* 73, no. 1 (1964), that reference to the institution of promising enables one to pass from a description of what people do to an account of what they ought to do. This controversial claim has led to much irrelevant criticism of his wider argument. All that is necessary for the wider argument is the recognition that people collectively undertake, accept, and rely upon obligations, not that those obligations exist as binding moral imperatives regardless of the collective belief in them.

so they create a realm of institutions and laws in which they find themselves more at home than they could ever be in a state of nature. Human beings create obligations by declaring them, and these obligations exist, Searle argues, objectively, as "deontic powers" that structure the world of institutions. You can see this theory as a first step toward fleshing out Husserl's idea of the *Lebenswelt*, showing just how it is that the human world can differ so radically from the world of animals, even though it contains, from the scientific point of view, only the same basic things.

The Order of the Covenant

It is a distinctive feature of the Jewish religious tradition that it regards the relation between God and his people as founded on a covenant—in other words, a binding agreement, in which God commands obedience only by putting himself under obligations toward those whom he commands. The idea that God can be bound by obligations toward his creation has had a profound impact on our civilization, since it implies that God's relation to us is of the same kind as the relations that we create through our promises and contracts. Our relation to God is a relation between free beings, who take responsibility for their actions. And the simplest form that such a relation can take is that of an exchange of promises—a form that has been recognized by the law since ancient times.[2] When one person elicits a promise in exchange for a promise, he is under an obligation that can, in the right circumstances, be enforced at law.

Through the law of contract human beings have come to understand the logic of such obligations. This is something that they have managed without the benefit of academic philosophy, by eliciting principles that seem to be implied in the very idea of promising, and which are followed whenever people attempt to settle their disputes before an impartial judge. Although different systems of contract law exist—the Roman and the English, for example—their differences

---

[2] For example, by the Babylonian code of Hammurabi (1792–1750 BC), which contains provisions governing contract, liability, and tort.

result, either from views about the nature and status of people (most ancient laws discriminating between freemen and slaves), or from the fact that governments or interest groups try to achieve goals that are independent of anything implied in the contractual agreement. For example, governments might grant security of tenure to tenants under rental agreements, regardless of the terms of the agreement. The usual result of this attempt to adjust the rights of contractual partners according to some independent agenda is that contracts of the relevant kind cease to exist—as rental contracts, for example, were effectively destroyed by the UK Rent Act of 1968, which granted security of tenure at controlled rents. This is because people do not enter into contracts when the obligations transcend those that they are consciously undertaking.

Hence the common law of contract exhibits forms of reasoning that exist everywhere, even in societies which do not have written systems of law, and even in places like children's playgrounds where law is simply the collectively enforced institution of fair play. Here are some of the principles that are everywhere acknowledged: a contract entered into by force or fraud is not enforceable. A contract is valid only if made with a responsible adult, and only if the terms are clear and clearly understood. Contracts are to be honored, and a person who obtains a benefit under a contract is obliged to fulfill his part of it. A person in breach of a contract is obliged to compensate the other party, by putting him so far as possible in the position that he would have been in had the contract been fulfilled. A person who contracts to receive some benefit or good is entitled to a true description of the item he is to acquire. Those and other principles, which flow immediately from the nature of human agreements, provide the foundations of the "natural law" upon which Hugo Grotius drew, in developing the law of nations.[3]

The field of tort, or injury, is similar, in generating shared principles that seem to be implicit in our mutual dealings. Tort is not about the deontic consequences of agreement, but about the assignment of liability when the actions of one person damage the interests of

---

[3] Grotius, *De jure belli ac pacis* (Paris, 1625); English edition, edited by Richard Tuck as *The Rights of War and Peace*, bks. 1–3 (Indianapolis, IN: Liberty Fund, 2005).

another. Like the law of contract the common law of tort is a treasure trove of ordinary practical reasoning, which shows the inherent structure of liabilities as they arise spontaneously in ordinary relations of dependence. This point was evident to J. L. Austin, who devotes some of his most important papers to concepts that arise in the course of common-law reasoning—notably the concept of excuses, through which we come to understand the distinction between the consequences of a person's actions that can be *imputed* to him, and the consequences that arise through no fault of his own. The concept of imputation played a vital part in Kant's account of legal reasoning in part 1 of *The Metaphysic of Morals* (entitled "The Science of Right"), and Austin's arguments in "A Plea for Excuses" and "Ifs and Cans" can be seen as reworking the ground covered by Kant and others in the eighteenth century.[4] The basic point is that we impute to persons all those consequences of their actions or inactions that can be brought within the sphere of first-person awareness and free choice—which they can account for as "mine," and for which they can be *called* to account as "your doing."

This observation reminds us that the world of obligations and rights is not an artificial imposition designed to serve the purpose of some sovereign power, but rather the natural outgrowth of the I-You encounter. Jurists like Samuel Pufendorf and Hugo Grotius were not simply expounding the technicalities of Roman law. To them that was a secondary activity, which made sense only in the context of a more general account of the natural principles through which human beings bind themselves in obligations, acknowledge rights, enforce agreements, and resolve disputes. Likewise, Adam Smith's account of morality, in terms of the considered judgment of the "impartial spectator," is a generalization of principles that underpin not only ordinary moral discourse but also the common law. And he summarizes the principle of contract, in his lectures on jurisprudence, as issuing directly from the obligation contained in a promise. If openly and

---

[4] J. L. Austin, "Ifs and Cans" and "A Plea for Excuses," in *Philosophical Papers* (Oxford: Clarendon Press, 1955). Kant, *The Metaphysic of Morals*, trans. and ed. Mary Gregor (Cambridge: Cambridge University Press, 1996), pt. 1. Kant was writing before the term "responsibility" (*Verantwortung*) had become current in legal and moral parlance. He referred instead to the Roman-law concept of "imputatio," which he translates as *Zurechnung*.

clearly declared, he argues, a promise induces the reasonable expectation that it will be acted upon. This expectation is such "as an impartial spectator would readily go along with," as Smith puts it,[5] and it is this that makes contracts binding, even when there is no legal apparatus to enforce them. In all our dealings we are not only I and you but also he or she: in other words, an agent in the eyes of the spectator, an object of judgment, including judgment made by ourselves. And this too is the inescapable result of the I-You relation. In seeing myself as a you in your eyes, I am lifted outside myself, to adopt the attitude of the spectator: and I demand the same of you. The impartial spectator comes into being as a kind of shadow of our relations; he is "the third who walks always beside you," in whose eyes we are both being judged. This sentiment too "overreaches" itself, and points to the horizon of our world. Nor should this surprise us. For the sense that we are judged in all our dealings is the heart of religion.

The Calculus of Rights

If we follow that argument through, it seems to me, we will arrive at the ancient concept of natural law: the concept of a law inscribed in human reason itself, and which issues precisely from our disposition to bind ourselves in free agreements and to live with our neighbors on terms. There is, as I prefer to put it, a "calculus of rights, responsibilities, and duties" that is inherent in our search for agreement, and this calculus lays down the constraints that must be obeyed, if we are to arrive at a consensual political order. It is from the workings of this calculus that we can derive a viable conception of human rights.[6]

We owe much in this area to W. N. Hohfeld,[7] whose typology of legal rights and obligations brought order into the discussion. Hohfeld was dealing not with natural rights, but with rights as defined by a

[5] *Lectures on Jurisprudence* (Indianapolis, IN: Liberty Press, 2001), p. 87.

[6] I have spelled this out at greater length in *Animal Rights and Wrongs* (London: Continuum, 2004), in which I argue that, properly understood, the concept of a right is dependent on self-consciousness, so that, in the normal understanding of the term, animals do not have rights—which does not mean that we can treat them as we wish.

[7] W. N. Hohfeld, *Fundamental Legal Conceptions as Applied in Judicial Reasoning* (New Haven, CT: Yale University Press, 1923).

legal system, and he distinguished claim rights from liberty rights, and both from powers on the one hand and immunities on the other. It is the first two of those, and the distinction between them, that is of principal concern in the discussion of human rights. A claim right typically arises from some past circumstance that creates a claim by one person against another who is bound to honor it. For example, if I have transferred to you my house in accordance with a contract of sale, then I have a claim against you for the agreed price, and this is a claim right of mine—in other words, a claim that would be upheld in a court of law, should any dispute arise. Claim rights also arise in tort. If your negligently allowing your cows onto my lawn causes five hundred dollars' worth of damage, then I have a claim right against you, for that sum.

In those straightforward cases of contract and tort, we easily see that every claim right in one person defines a duty in the other. Indeed, Hohfeld defines a claim right as a "directed duty"—a duty directed toward the particular person who has the claim. And this duty is a legal burden. Often it cannot be discharged: the person claimed against may not have the means to satisfy the claim. However, he ought to satisfy it, and the law will compel him to do so to the best of his power. Furthermore, the duty that the law imposes arises from a relationship of responsibility. Both in contract and in tort—as well as in trust—the law holds someone *liable* for a claim made by another. And this liable person is identified, either as an individual, or as a company or a group, that has acted so as to *incur* the liability in question. Hence there can be no calculus of rights and duties that does not also involve a procedure of "imputation." That procedure defines the legal meaning of "responsibility."

Claim rights, in the normal cases, are quite different from freedom rights. A freedom right imposes a general duty on others to observe it; but it may arise from no specific relationship, and may make no specific demands of any individual. It is a right that is violated by an act of intrusion or invasion, but which is respected by doing nothing. The duty to observe a freedom right is therefore neither onerous nor a special responsibility of any particular person. Such is my right to life, limb, and property, and the other rights traditionally acknowledged as flowing from the natural law. You respect them by

noninvasion, and the duty to respect them falls clearly and unam-
biguously on everyone.

This does not mean that there are no legal difficulties over enforc-
ing freedom rights, or that special relations may not bear on them.
For one thing, freedom rights can conflict: as when my freedom to
grow vegetables in my garden conflicts with your freedom to plant a
leylandii hedge next to it. The law takes the sensible view that freedoms of this kind are not unqualified, and that the conflicts can be
resolved by inserting the qualifications. Nevertheless, if you really
have a right to do something, then you are wronged by any judgment that forbids you to do it. A conflict of rights, which cannot be
resolved by qualification, is strictly analogous to a moral dilemma, in
which one is obliged to perform two incompatible courses of action.
This absolute nature of rights should not be misunderstood. Rights
define what Joseph Raz has called exclusionary reasons—that is, reasons whose validity excludes countervailing arguments—not overriding reasons, that is, reasons which must prevail.[8] My right to close
my door against you is breached by your decision to break it down.
However, unknown to me, but observed by you, a fire has broken out
on the second floor and you are breaking in to fight it. In such a case
your moral duty to save my life overrides my right to exclude you.
Nevertheless, your decision to break down my door is a violation of a
right, and I am to that extent wronged by your action.

Rights Inflation

Claim rights arise in contract and tort—as Hohfeld recognizes. I
doubt that, in Hohfeld's day, there was any legal recognition afforded
to claims against everyone by anyone, regardless of the relation between the parties. However, this is the kind of right that has begun
to creep into the lists of supposed "human rights" proposed by trans-
national legislatures. The switch from freedom rights to claim rights
is made easier by the ambiguity of many formulations. Take the right

---

[8]Joseph Raz, *The Authority of Law: Essays on Law and Morality* (Oxford: Oxford University
Press, 1979).

to life. As proposed in the American Declaration of Independence this meant the freedom to go about my business without threat to my life. It imposes on others the duty not to kill me, and since this is a duty under any moral understanding, and one that Kant, for example, held to be justifiable a priori, there is no intellectual difficulty in including the right to life among the list of natural rights.

However, the phrase "right to life" can easily be inflected so as to acquire another meaning, as the right to be protected against anything that threatens to take my life away—disease, for example. A person with a life-threatening illness might, on this understanding, be construed as suffering a breach in his rights. And if we put it that way, we are immediately saddled with the question of duty: whose is the duty to help him, and how? Suppose there is a doctor somewhere who can cure the disease, but who is too tired, too far away, too fed up with unpaid demands on his time, and so on, and who therefore does not respond to the call for help. We might reproach this doctor. But do we want to go along with the claim-right understanding of the phrase, and say that he has violated another's "right to life"? At the very least we can see that this is controversial in a way that the freedom-right understanding of the phrase is not. We surely have other, and better, ways of describing the duties involved in cases like this, ways which do not place the kind of absolute claim on another's conduct that is implied in the language of rights.

Now it is easy to see why a libertarian might object to the expansion of the list of human rights to include claim rights—especially claims to nonspecific benefits like health, education, a certain standard of living, and so on, many of which crept into the Universal Declaration of Human Rights with the approval of Eleanor Roosevelt. For, in the absence of any relation of liability, specifying who is to satisfy these claims, they inevitably point to the state as the only possible provider. And large, vague claims require a massive expansion of state power, a surrender to the state of all kinds of responsibilities that previously vested in individuals, and the centralization of social life in the government machine. In other words, claim rights push us inevitably in a direction that, for many people, is morally and politically dangerous. Moreover, it is a direction that is diametrically opposed to that for which the idea of a human (natural) right was originally introduced—a direction involving the increase, rather than the limitation, of the power of the state.

But there is another reason for disquiet over the idea that claim rights might also be human rights. Hohfeld's argument suggests that the concept of a right belongs in a family of concepts—liability, immunity, duty, permission, power, and so on—which are like modal concepts, such as possibility, necessity, and probability, in identifying interlocking operations of rational thought. The concept of a right belongs to what one might call (in deference to Quine) a "circle of juridical terms," which are intricately interdefinable, and which between them specify a systematic operation of the rational intellect.[9] There is, to repeat, a "calculus of rights, responsibilities, and duties," which rational beings use in order to settle their disputes and to reach agreement over matters of common or conflicting interest. The availability of this calculus is one of the things that distinguish us from the lower animals, and it would be available to us even if we did not attempt to back it up with a shared legal system. The concept of justice belongs to this calculus: injustice resides in the denial of rights and deserts, as in undeserved punishment, theft, oppression, enslavement, and false witness.

The Grounding of Rights

There is an interesting philosophical question as to how this "rights talk" is grounded. And there is another question, partly philosophical, partly anthropological, as to the *function* of rights talk. Why do human beings make use of juridical terms? What do they gain from it, and why has it stabilized in so many different parts of the world, so as to be received as entirely natural? I should like to venture an answer to those questions. It seems to me that rights talk has the function of enabling people to claim a sphere of personal sovereignty, in which their choice is law. And spheres of personal sovereignty in turn have a function, namely, that they enable us to undertake

[9] See W. V. Quine, "Two Dogmas of Empiricism," in *From a Logical Point of View* (Cambridge, MA: MIT Press, 1956), on the "circle of intensional terms."

obligations freely—in other words to create the realm of institutional facts that Searle emphasizes in his social philosophy. Hence they give the advantage to consensual relations. They define the boundaries behind which people can retreat and which cannot be crossed without transgression.

The primary function of the idea of a right, therefore, is to identify something as within the boundary of me and mine. If I have a right to sit in a certain room, then you cannot expel me from it without wronging me. By determining such rights, we define the fixed points, the places of security, from which people can negotiate and agree. Without those fixed points negotiation and free agreement are unlikely to occur, and if they occur, their outcome is unlikely to be stable. If I have no rights, then the agreement between us provides no guarantee of performance; my sphere of action is liable to constant invasion by others, and there is nothing that I can do to define the position from which I am negotiating in a way that compels you to acknowledge it.

Rights, then, enable us to establish a society in which consensual relations are the norm, and they do this by defining for each of us the sphere of personal sovereignty from which others are excluded. This explains Dworkin's view, in *Taking Rights Seriously*, that "rights are trumps."[10] A right is part of the fence that defines my sovereign territory: by claiming it, I put an absolute veto on things that you might do. It also explains the direct connection between right and duty: the absoluteness of the right is tantamount to a duty to respect it. And it explains the zero-sum nature of disputes in a court of law, when rights are invoked to decide them.

If we look at rights in this way, as instruments that safeguard sovereignty, and so make free deals between sovereign partners into the cement of society, then we see immediately why freedom rights have the best claim to universality, and why claim rights—detached from any history of responsibility and agreement—present a threat to the consensual order. A claim against another, if expressed as a right, is an imposition of a duty. If this duty arises from no free action or chain of responsibility that would provide a cogent ground for the claim, then

[10]Ronald Dworkin, *Taking Rights Seriously* (Cambridge, MA: Harvard University Press, 1978).

by expressing it as a right we override the other's sovereignty. We say to him: here is something you must do or provide, even though your duty to do so arises from nothing you have done or for which you are responsible. This is simply a demand that you must satisfy. And that, in turn, seems like an invasion of his rights.

How different such a case is, at least, from that of freedom rights. For these are by their very nature "sovereignty protecting" devices. They are vetoes on what others can do to me or take from me, rather than demands that they do something or give something in which I have an interest. The duty that they define is one of noninterference, and the interest that they protect is the most fundamental interest that I have, namely, my interest in retaining the power to make decisions for myself in those matters that most closely concern me. Freedom rights exist to ensure that we can each appear in the public realm as free subjects, so as to engage in those I-You relations upon which the public realm is ultimately founded. The concept of a right is therefore grounded in the kind of metaphysics of the self that I defended in the previous two chapters. It is a fundamental instrument of human understanding, defining a well-trodden path of conflict and conciliation in the *Lebenswelt*.

Justice and Freedom

If there are such things as "natural rights," therefore, they ought to have the essentially negative aspect of freedoms: rights not to be molested, rather than claims to specific benefits. But no such limitation is acknowledged by the bodies that pretend to declare human rights in modern conditions. Bentham's view of the concept of natural rights, as "nonsense upon stilts," was the first conscious recognition of the danger represented by "rights inflation," the danger that people might claim as a right, and on no legal authority, what is merely an interest, and so block the road to negotiation and compromise. The concept of a human right was supposed to provide a neutral standpoint *outside* legal and moral controversies, from which the legitimacy of any particular decision can be evaluated. In fact it is now used to *take sides* in political controversies. And since nobody who makes use of the conception, so far as I can see, ever asks how a right can be justified, I cannot help feeling that they have no greater trust in the notion than Jeremy Bentham had.

Assuming, however, the kind of limitation of the doctrine of rights that I have been suggesting, we can begin to explore a vital distinction in human affairs, between those matters that are governed by justice, and those that depend upon some other form of bond between people. Aristotle defined justice as giving to each person his due. In other (and more modern) words, justice means respecting rights and deserts. Justice is a side constraint on human relations that governs our cooperative enterprises. It is a property of human actions and omissions, and is largely understood negatively, through the various ways in which we commit injustices—a point that is again made clear by Adam Smith, and also by Kant. I commit an injustice when I override or ignore another's sovereignty, by refusing to acknowledge his rights or deserts in a matter that concerns him, for example by dictating to him, or refusing to solicit his agreement, or defrauding him by lies and trickery. In the celebrated passage of *The Phenomenology of Spirit* to which I have already referred, Hegel suggests that in all of us there is a kind of residue of relations of domination and servitude, and that our disposition to seek the I-You encounter, in which free agreement and open acknowledgment of the other replaces dictatorship, has emerged from and bears the traces of the "life-and-death struggles" that preceded the emergence of negotiation and law. This thought of Hegel's (which peeps through Girard's account of sacrifice that I briefly discussed in chapter 1) seems to me to be entirely persuasive, and one way of expressing it is to say that justice is the fulfillment of human freedom—the form of human relations in which obligations are freely undertaken, and objectively binding *for the very reason* that they are freely undertaken. And we *win through* to justice by adopting in our mutual dealings the standpoint of the impartial judge.

It is perhaps worth pointing out two important consequences that follow from seeing justice in this way: first, the distinction between the just and the unjust is internal to everyday practical reasoning, and can be understood and agreed to by all of us; second, it is a distinction within the realm of human action, and does not apply to states of affairs judged as they are in themselves, and without reference to how they came about. It is therefore at variance with the approach to justice advanced in recent times by John Rawls and others, which sees justice as a property of distributions and outcomes. The dispute here is deep and difficult. But let me say only that, if we look at justice in Rawls's way, we weaken the connection between justice and responsibility, and remove the concept of justice from our ordinary practical reasoning. It is precisely the emphasis on outcomes, rather than actions, obligations, and responsibilities, that has led to the overriding of ordinary contract and tort with legislation aimed at redistributing rewards. Hence the constantly growing list of "human rights" that have no grounding in our ordinary free dealings, but which exist to achieve some overarching political purpose.

Noncontractual Obligations

I won't go further into that area, since it concerns the deep dispute in our time between socialists and classical liberals concerning the good government of modern societies—a dispute that would be the theme of another book. Instead I want to explore the ways in which the human world reaches *beyond* the boundaries of justice, toward obligations that are bequeathed and bestowed, rather than created. I am skeptical of the attempts to expand the concept of justice, so as to include the many claims made on behalf of it by socialists and their fellow travelers. However, I agree with the left-liberal consensus, that we are encumbered by more obligations than those we have explicitly contracted, and that free choice is not the only material from which the realm of duties is built. As I shall later argue, the order of the covenant requires us to reach beyond it, so as to assume obligations that do not have their origin in our consent to them.

Thus many of the relations that are most important to us cannot be captured by the terms of a contract: affection, friendship, love all reach beyond the bounds of mere agreement, to involve a kind of unconditional giving to the other that might expect reciprocity but does not demand it. In effect, although many of the deontic powers by which we are surrounded are created in the way that Searle suggests, we also find ourselves subject to bonds and obligations that are "transcendent," in that they seem neither to arise from, nor to be extinguished by, agreements between living people. These bonds and obligations are endowed with an "eternal" character. They lack clear temporal boundaries, and the ability to recognize and act on them is fundamental not only to the religious way of life, but also to the full elaboration of the *Lebenswelt*.

We can understand what is at issue here in terms of three contrasts—that between a contract and a vow, that between justice and piety, and that between affection and love. A contract has terms, which define the agreement. When the terms are fulfilled, the contract is at an end; if they are not fulfilled but breached, then the obligation to perform is changed into an obligation to compensate. Fraudulent contracts, coerced agreements, or contracts that are escaped when the innocent party has fulfilled his undertaking are paradigm cases of injustice—in such a case one person treats another as a mere instrument, and tramples on his rights. Vows, by contrast, may not have precise terms, and are open-ended commitments to make oneself trustworthy in a certain respect. They have an existential character, in that they tie their parties together in a shared destiny and what was once called a "substantial unity."

To put the point in another way, a vow is a self-dedication, a gift of oneself, either wholly or partly, on which the other is being invited to rely. The paradigm case of this is marriage, as it was conceived until recent times, and as it is still conceived in many communities around the world. The traditional marriage, seen from the external perspective as a rite of passage to another social condition, is seen from within as a vow. This vow may be preceded by a promise. But it is something more than a promise, since the obligations to which it leads cannot be spelled out in finite terms. A vow of marriage creates an existential tie, not a set of specifiable obligations. And the gradual vanishing of marital vows is one special case of the transition "from status to contract" that was discussed, from the external perspective, by that great armchair anthropologist Sir Henry Maine.[11] But there is also more to the change than that. The triumph of the contractual view of marriage represents a change in the phenomenology of sexual

[11] Sir Henry Maine, *Ancient Law* (Oxford: Clarendon Press, 1861).

union, a retreat from the world of "substantial ties" to a world of negotiated deals. And the world of vows is a world of sacred things, in
which holy and indefeasible obligations stand athwart our lives and
command us along certain paths, whether we will or not. It is this
experience that the church has always tried to safeguard, and it is one
that has been jeopardized by the state, in its efforts to refashion marriage for a secular age.

Now, institutions like marriage are relatively easy to understand
from the external point of view—the view of the functionalist anthropologist. Marriage is a rite of passage—an event in the life of the individual, which is also an event in the life of the community, an event
in which some of the community's will to live is invested. The community has an interest in insisting that the bond of marriage is more
than a contract, and in imposing on the partners the kind of existential
commitment that will safeguard the future of any children that issue
from the marriage. Communities which no longer insist on that commitment, or which allow the erosion of marriage first by its rewriting
as a contract and then as a choice which parents may or may not choose
to make, are communities that offer no security to their children.

But it is not the external justification of marriage that concerns me:
rather its internal logic, what it is from the point of view of those who
enter it. A vow is like a contract in being the voluntary undertaking of
free beings. But it is unlike a contract in having no delimited terms,
and in stretching forward indefinitely in time. It has a "transcendent"
character, and this feature is often registered by the participants in an
invitation or a summons to the gods. You call the gods as witness to a
vow, and thereby give to your undertaking a different kind of permanence than could attach to any contract—it is written in the heavens,
or inscribed in runes on Wotan's spear.[12] Another way of expressing
this point is to say that vows, at least of the relation-forming kind,
have a *sacramental* quality. Sacred beings are present at their incep-
tion and oversee their course. This can be witnessed in all the rites
of passage that are familiar to us—although it has been controversial

---

[12] To be burned away, in time, by Loge's fire. Moreover, when the spear at last is shattered
by the impetuous freedom of the self-affirming individual, all vows and all pious obligations
crumble to dust—such is the fate of the human world in *Götterdämmerung*.

in Christianity, and one of the points at issue between Catholic and Protestant, whether marriage is really to be regarded as a sacrament, comparable to baptism and Holy Communion.

The second contrast that interests me is that between justice and piety. An obligation of justice is owed to another because he has a right to it, or because he deserves it. Rights and deserts are comparable but not identical privileges: rights are, on the whole, positive benefits to the one who holds them, whereas deserts can be negative, as in a deserved punishment. If all our obligations arose from *undertakings*, in the manner supposed by Searle, then it would be natural to assume that they are all obligations of justice. But this is not so. There are obligations of piety—obligations that have never been undertaken but which are owed to others in recognition of their entitlement, or in gratitude for their protection, or simply as a humble acknowledgment that we are not the authors of our fate.

In *Leviathan* Thomas Hobbes defended a social contract theory of political obligation on the ground that "a man is under no obligation that ariseth not from some act of his own."[13] This idea has had a long subsequent history: it seems to justify political obedience in the same terms as justify the keeping of promises—namely, that citizens *put themselves under* the obligation to obey. But it is surely evident that some of the most important of our obligations are not undertaken in this way: for example, the obligation to parents. Hegel plausibly argues that the obligations of family life belong to the sphere of piety (the *lares et penates* of Roman religion), and that something is similar of political obligation too. Again, without arguing the point, I take it as evident that a complete account of human obligation must acknowledge piety as a distinct source of the "desire-independent reasons" that govern our duties.

Finally, the contrast between affection and love. In the *Nicomachean Ethics* Aristotle pointed out that friendships are of several kinds, and singled out three for particular attention—friendships of pleasure, of business, and of virtue, corresponding to three kinds of reasons for action (the pleasing, the useful, and the good). All of these come under the general heading of *philia*, as opposed to *eros*, and both

---

[13] Hobbes, *Leviathan*, pt. 2, chap. 21.

philia and *eros* are to be distinguished from the love advocated in the gospels under the name of *agape*, traditionally translated as charity or neighbor love. All of these relations create obligations, but only rarely can the obligations be translated into contractual terms. Moreover, the language of obligation does not capture what is special about our loves, namely, that they cannot be generalized. I can have general duties of charity, of business partnership, of neighborly goodwill— duties that do not demand that a *specific* person be acknowledged as their target. But love involves attachment to an individual, whose presence and well-being are integral to the identity of the one who loves—part of the ground of his being, to use the theological phrase. Hence love—properly understood—fills the world with another kind of necessity than that deriving from the obligations of charity and neighborliness. People find themselves bound by *nontransferable* attachments. These attachments invest the other with a unique value and distinguish him from all others in the universe. People find their fulfillment in this way, by discovering objects of attention and affection for which *there are no substitutes*.

Beyond the Covenant

Now, if we put together those three ideas, recognizing that human beings, as persons, do not live only in a world of contracts, but also in a world of vows, pious duties, and nonsubstitutable attachments, we arrive at another aspect of interpersonal cognition, and one that distances that form of cognition yet further from the scientific worldview. We cannot live in full personal communication with our kind if we treat all our relations as contractual. People are not for sale: to address the other as you rather than as he or she is automatically to see him or her as an individual for whom no substitutes exist. In the relations that really matter, others do not stand before me as members of an equivalence class. I endow them, in my feelings, with a kind of individuality that cannot be represented in the language of science, but which demands the use of concepts that would not feature in the commonsense scheme of things: concepts like those of the sacrificial and the sacramental.

Another way of putting this point is in terms of the idea of a "transcendent bond." Not all our obligations are freely undertaken, and created by choice. Some we receive "from outside the will." They are marked by two features: their long-term social function, and their lack of internal plasticity. Vows of marriage, obligations toward parents and children, sacred ties to home and country: such things have to be rescued from the corrosions of the will, made inflexible and "eternal," if they are to perform their manifest function, of securing society against the forces of selfish desire. It is hardly surprising, therefore, if they are wound into the eternal order of things by moments of sacrificial awe.

Much has been written about the social effects of secularization. But it seems to me that the crucial point has yet to be properly expressed, which is that the principal effect has been on the *Lebenswelt*. The world of obligations has been steadily remade as a world of contracts, and therefore of obligations that are rescindable, finite, and dependent upon individual choice. Burke long ago made the point, in opposition to Rousseau's social contract theory and its subversive effect, namely, that if society is a contract, then it is one to which the dead, the living, and the unborn are all equally partners: in other words, not a contract at all, but an inheritance of trusteeship, which cannot be reduced to the agreement to be bound by it.[14] All obligations of love are like that.

The process of secularization can be understood from the example of Rousseau. It involves clearing away from the *Lebenswelt* all the threads of pious observance that cannot be replaced by free choice and self-made obligations. The world is remade without the transcendental reference, without the encounter with sacred things, without the vows of allegiance and submission, which have no other justification than the weight of inherited duty. But it turns out—and this is what I shall try to show in the chapters that follow—that those vows were far more deeply woven into the fabric of our experience than enlightened people tend to think, and that the world without transcendent bonds is not a variant of the world that had not yet been cleansed of them, but a completely different world, and one in which

---

[14]Edmund Burke, *Reflections on the Revolution in France* (1791).

we humans are not truly at home. Such at least is my claim. If true it tells us something extremely important about religious experience, and about the transformation of the world that comes about when we cease to relate its meaning to a transcendental source. In all durable societies, I maintain, the order of the covenant is overreached into another order, in which obligations are transcendent, attachments sacred, and contracts dissolved in vows.

5

Facing Each Other

The beauty that is borne here in the face
The bearer knows not, but commends itself
To others' eyes: nor doth the eye itself,
That most pure spirit of sense, behold itself,
Not going from itself; but eye to eye opposed
Salutes each other with each other's form;
For speculation turns not to itself,
Till it hath travell'd and is mirror'd there
Where it may see itself. This is not strange at all.
(Shakespeare, *Troilus and Cressida*)

The facts conjured by Shakespeare in those lines are indeed not strange, for they are the constantly repeated refrain of personal life. But as soon as we examine them, we discover them to be as strange as anything we know. I have suggested that our way of understanding the person employs concepts that have no part to play in the explanatory sciences, and situates people—both self and other—in some way on the edge of things. People are objects in the world of objects, certainly. But we address them as subjects, each with its own distinctive perspective on the world, and each addressing the world from its own horizon. There is a mystery that attaches to the subject, though it is not a mystery that could ever be solved by the ontological dualism of the Cartesians. The mystery is that of the "real presence." How can this thing that is not a thing but a perspective, *appear* in the world of objects where it occupies no place? How is it that we can not only address the other, but actually encounter him in the empirical world? The answer is suggested by the fact that each of us shows his face in that world, and the face, although it appears in the world of objects, belongs essentially to the subject.

I have discussed this topic in *The Face of God*, and here I summarize some of the theses defended at greater length in that book. The concept of the face, I argue, belongs with those of freedom and responsibility as part of the interpersonal understanding of the world. That is to say, in seeing an array of features as a face, I do not understand it biologically, as the visible film that encases another brain and lets in, through eyes and ears, the information that the brain is processing. I understand it as the real presence in our shared world of *you*.

My face is also the part of me to which others direct their attention, whenever they address me as "you." I lie *behind* my face, and yet I am present in it, speaking and looking through it at a world of others who are in turn both revealed and concealed like me. My face is a boundary, a threshold, a place where I appear as the monarch appears on the balcony of the palace. (Thus Dante, in the *Convivio*, describes the eyes and the mouth as "balconies of the soul.") My face is therefore bound up with the pathos of my condition. In a sense you are always more clearly aware than I can be of what I am *in* the world; and when I confront my own face, there may be a moment of fear, as I try to fit the person whom I know so well to this thing that others know better. How can the person, whom I know as a continuous unity from my earliest days until now, be identical with this decaying flesh that others have addressed through all its changes? This is the question that Rembrandt explored in his lifelong series of self-portraits. For Rembrandt the face is the place where the self and the flesh melt together, and where the individual is revealed not only in the life that shines on the surface but also in the death that is growing in the folds. The Rembrandt self-portrait is that rare thing—a portrait of the self. It shows the subject incarnate in the object, embraced by its own mortality, and present like death on the unknowable edge of things.

When I confront Mary face-to-face, I am not confronting a physical part of her, as I am when, for example, I look at her shoulder or her knee. I am confronting *her*, the individual center of consciousness, the free being who reveals herself in the face as another like me. Hence there are deceiving faces, but not deceiving elbows or knees. When I read a face, I am in some way acquainting myself with the way things seem to another person. The face occurs in the world of objects as though lit from behind. Hence it becomes the target and expression of our interpersonal attitudes, and looks, glances, smiles become the currency of our affections.

This means that the human face has a kind of inherent ambiguity. It can be seen in two ways—as the vehicle for the subjectivity that shines in it, and as a part of the human anatomy. The tension here comes to the fore in eating, as has been argued by Leon Kass and Raymond Tallis.[1] We do not, as animals do, thrust our mouths into our food in order to ingest it. We lift the food to our mouths, while retaining the upright posture that enables us to converse with our neighbors. In all societies (prior to the present) eating is a social occasion, with a pronounced ritual character, often preceded by a prayer of thanks. It occurs in a space that has been sanctified and ritualized, and into which the gods have been invited. All rituals impose discipline on the face, and this is part of what we experience when eating. Even when serving a biological purpose, my face remains under my jurisdiction. It is the place where I am in the world of objects, and the place from which I address you.

Smiling, Looking, Kissing, Blushing

Hence the face has an interesting repertoire of adjustments, which cannot be understood merely as physical changes of the kind that we observe in the features of other species. For example, there is smiling. Animals do not smile: at best they grimace, in the manner of chimpanzees and bonobos. In *Paradise Lost*, Milton writes (describing the love between Adam and Eve) that "smiles from reason flow, / To brute denied, and are of love the food." The smile that reveals is the involuntary smile, the blessing that one soul confers upon another, when shining with the whole self in a moment of self-revelation. The voluntary and deliberately amplified smile is not a smile but a mask. The "smiley face" that all children know how to draw is not the portrait of a smile. A face can smile only when the soul shines from it, and the geometrical smile is not a smile but a grin.

[1] Kass, *The Hungry Soul*; Raymond Tallis, *Hunger* (London: Acumen, 2008).

Whereas a sincere smile is involuntary, a sincere kiss is willed. That is true, at least, of the kiss of affection. In the kiss of erotic passion, however, the will is also in part overcome, and in this context the *purely* willed kiss has an air of *in*sincerity. The sincere erotic kiss is both an expression of will and a mutual surrender. Hence it requires a kind of government of the mouth, so that the soul can breathe out from it, and also surrender there, on the perimeter of one's being.

The erotic kiss is not a matter of lips only: still more are the eyes and the hands involved. The kiss of desire brings into prominence the very same ambiguity in the face that is present in eating. The lips offered by one lover to another are replete with subjectivity: they are the avatars of I, summoning the consciousness of another in a mutual gift. But although the lips are offered as spirit, they respond as flesh. Pressed by the lips of the other, they become sensory organs, bringing with them all the fatal entrapment of sexual pleasure, and ready to surrender to a force that breaks into the I from outside. Hence the kiss is the most important moment of desire—the moment in which lovers are fully face-to-face and also totally exposed to one another. The pleasure of the kiss is a matter not of sensations, but of the I-You intentionality and what it means. Kisses have an aboutness of their own. Hence there can be mistaken kisses, and mistaken pleasure in kissing, as was experienced by Lucretia, in Benjamin Britten and Ronald Duncan's version of the story, kissing the man she thought to be her husband, and whom she discovered to be the rapist Tarquin, though too late to defend herself.

The presence of the subject in the face is yet more evident in the eyes, and eyes play their part in both smiles and looks. Animals can look at things: they also look at each other. But they do not look *into* things. Perhaps the most concentrated of all acts of nonverbal communication between people is that of lovers, when they look into each other's eyes. They are not looking at the retina, or exploring the eye for its anatomical peculiarities, as an optician might. So what are they looking at or looking for? The answer is surely obvious: each is looking for, and hoping also to be looking at, the other, as a free subjectivity who is striving to meet him I to I. In his seminal discussion in *L'Être et le néant* of the gaze (*le regard*) Sartre makes abundantly clear that the look bestowed on another subject is itself a revelation of the subject—it has the overreaching intentionality that I described in chapter 3. That is why the gaze of another person is disturbing. It is an intrusion into the world from a point beyond its horizon, and a summons to me to account for myself as a free subjectivity.

To turn my eyes to you is a voluntary act. But what I then receive from you is not of my doing. As the symbol of all perception the eyes come to stand for that "epistemic transparency" which enables the person to be revealed to another in his embodiment—as we are revealed in our looks, smiles, and blushes. The joining of perspective that is begun when a glance is answered with a blush or a smile finds final realization in wholly reciprocated glances: the "me seeing you seeing me" of rapt attention, where neither of us can be said to be either doing or suffering what is done.

Looks are voluntary. But the full revelation of the subject in the face is not, as a rule, voluntary. Smiles are usually involuntary, and "gift smiles," as one might call them, always so. Likewise laughter, to be genuine, must be involuntary—even though laughter is something of which only creatures with intentions, reason, and self-consciousness are capable. The important point is that, while smiling and laughing are movements of the mouth, the whole face is infused by them, so that the subject is revealed in them as "overcome." Laughing and smiling can also be willed, and when they are willed, they have a ghoulish, threatening quality, as when someone laughs cynically, or hides behind a smile. Voluntary laughter is a kind of spiritual armor, with which a person defends himself against a treacherous world by betraying it.

Blushes are more like tears than like laughter in that they cannot be intended. Only a rational being can blush, even though nobody can blush voluntarily. Even if, by some trick, you are able to make the blood flow into the surface of your cheeks, this would not be blushing but a kind of deception. And it is the involuntary character of the blush that conveys its meaning, which resides in the fact that it is the *other* who summons it. Looks directed to the looks of another have an "interrogatory aboutness," so to speak. The person who looks at his companion is also aware that he is on the verge of looking *into* him. There is an element of overreaching here, which is inherited from the I-You encounter, and which changes the appearance of the human look in the eyes of the person looked at. Blushing is a natural response to this, a recognition that the glance that originated at the horizon where you are has touched the horizon in me.

Masking the Self

It is, I hope, not too fanciful to extend this phenomenology of the face a little further, and to see the face as a symbol of the individual and a display of his individuality. People are individual animals; but they are also individual persons, and as I argued in chapter 2, there is a puzzle as to how they can be both. On one tradition—that associated with Locke—the identity of the person through time is established by the continuity of the "I," and not by reference to the constancy of the body. Although I don't accept this, I do accept that being a person has something to do with the ability to remember the past and intend the future, while holding oneself accountable for both. And this connection between personality and the first-person case has in turn something to do with our sense that human beings are individuals of a special kind and in a special sense that distinguishes them from other spatiotemporal particulars. The knowledge that I have of my own individuality, which derives from my direct and criterionless awareness of the unity that binds my mental states, gives substance to the view that I am maintained in being as an individual, through all conceivable bodily change. My *Istigkeit* or *haecceitas* is exemplified in me, as something that I cannot lose. It is prior to all my states and properties and reducible to none of them. In this I am godlike too. And it is this inner awareness of absolute individuality that is translated into the face and there made flesh. The eyes that look at me are your eyes, and also you: the mouth that speaks and cheeks that blush are you.

The sense of the face as irradiated by the person and infused with his self-identity underlies the power of masks in the theater. In the classical theater of Greece, as in that of Japan, the mask was regarded not only as essential to the heightened tension of the drama, but also as the best way to guarantee that the emotions expressed by the words are reflected in the face. It is the spectator, gripped by the words, who sees their meaning shining in the mask. The impediment of human flesh has been removed, and the mask appears to change with every fluctuation of the character's emotions, to become the outward sign of inner feeling, precisely because the expression on the mask originates not so much in the one who wears it as in the one who beholds it. To make a mask that can be seen in this way requires skills acquired over a lifetime—perhaps more than a lifetime, the maskmakers of the Noh theater of Japan handing on their art over many generations, and the best of the masks being retained in the private collections of patrons and performers, to be brought out only on occasions of the greatest solemnity.

The mask was a symbol of Dionysus, the god at whose festival the tragedies were performed. It did not signify the god's remoteness from the spectators—Dionysus was no *deus absconditus*. It signified his real presence among them. Dionysus was the god of tragedy and also the god of rebirth, conveyed by the wine into the soul of his worshippers, so as to include them in the dance of his own resurrection. The mask was the face of the god, sounding on the stage with the voice of human suffering, and sounding in the mystery cult with a divine and dithyrambic joy.

It is significant that the word "person," which we borrow to express all those aspects of the human being associated with first-person awareness, came originally from the Roman theater, where *persona* denoted the mask worn by the actor, and hence, by extension, the character portrayed.[2] By borrowing the term, the Roman law signified that, in a certain sense, we come always masked before judgment. As Sir Ernest Barker once put it: "it is not the natural Ego which enters a court of law. It is a right-and-duty bearing person, created by the law, which appears before the law."[3] The face, like the person, is both product and producer of judgment. This suggests a thought to which I return, which is that personhood, like obligation, is brought into being by our use of that very concept.

---

[2] There are conflicting etymologies: some say the word comes from Latin *per-sonare*, to sound through, others that the root is Etruscan, deriving from the cult of Persephone, who was the principal subject of the Etruscan theater, where she had a role resembling that of Dionysus in the Attic theater.

[3] Sir Ernest Barker, introduction to Otto Gierke, *Natural Law and the Theory of Society 1500–1800*, trans. Barker (Cambridge: Cambridge University Press, 1934), p. lxxi.

We should recognize too that it is not only in the theater that masks are used. There are societies—that of Venice being the most singular—in which masks and masquerades have acquired complex functions that bring them into the very center of communal life, to become indispensable items of clothing, without which people feel naked, indecent, or out of place. In the Venetian Carnival the mask traditionally served two purposes: to cancel the everyday identity of the person, and also to create a new identity in its place—an identity *bestowed by the other.* Just as in the theater the mask wears the expression projected onto it by the audience, so in the Carnival does the mask acquire its personality from the people all around. Hence, far from cutting people off from each other, the collective act of masking makes each person the product of others' interest: the moment of Carnival becomes the highest form of "social effervescence," to use Durkheim's pregnant phrase. And maybe our everyday interactions are more "carnivalesque" than we care to believe, the result of a constant and creative imagining that behind each face lies something like *this*—namely, the inner unity with which we are acquainted and for which none of us has words.[4] That thought gives rise to another: that the individuality of the other resides *merely* in our way of seeing him, and has little or nothing to do with his way of *being.* We are again setting feet on the path followed by Spinoza, which leads to the conclusion that there are no true individuals, but only localized vortices in the one thing that is everything.

Desiring the Individual

I am inclined to the view that there is no answer to the question what makes me the individual that I am that is not a trivial assertion of identity. But I am also inclined to the view that the notion of an absolute individuality arises spontaneously from the most fundamental interpersonal relations. It is implied in all our attempts

---

[4]We owe the word "carnivalesque," used to describe a comprehensive attitude to reality, to Mikhail Bakhtin, *Rabelais and His World*, trans. Hélène Iswolsky (Bloomington: Indiana University Press, 1993).

at integrity and responsible living. And it is built into our way of perceiving as well as our way of describing the human world. Rather than dismiss it as an illusion, I would prefer to say that it is a "well-founded phenomenon," in Leibniz's sense, a way of seeing the world that is indispensable to us, and which we could never have conclusive reason to reject.

Moreover, the face has this meaning for us because it is the threshold at which the other appears, offering "this thing that I am" as a partner in dialogue. This feature goes to the heart of what it is to be human. Our interpersonal relations would be inconceivable without the assumption that we can commit ourselves through promises, take responsibility now for some event in the future or the past, make vows that bind us forever to the one who receives them, and undertake obligations that we regard as untransferable to anyone else. And all this we read in the face.

Especially do we read those things in the face of the beloved in the look of love. Our sexual emotions are founded on individualizing thoughts: it is *you* whom I want and not the type or pattern. This individualizing intentionality does not merely stem from the fact that it is persons (in other words, individuals) whom we desire. It stems from the fact that the other is desired as an embodied subject, and not as a body.[5] And the embodied subject is what we see in the face. I don't need to emphasize the extent to which our understanding of desire has been influenced and indeed subverted by the literature, from Havelock Ellis through Freud to the Kinsey reports, which has purported to lift the veil from our collective secrets. But it is worth pointing out that if you describe desire in the terms that have become fashionable—as the pursuit of pleasurable sensations in the private parts—then the sphere of sexual relations becomes entirely "demoralized." The outrage and pollution of rape, for example, then become impossible to explain. Rape, on this view, is every bit as bad as being spat upon: but no worse. In fact, just about everything in human sexual behavior becomes unintelligible—and it is only the "charm

---

[5] I have defended this point at length in *Sexual Desire: A Moral Philosophy of the Erotic* (New York: Free Press, 1986). The notion of the "embodied subject" is also fundamental to the analysis of perception given by Merleau-Ponty.

of disenchantment" that leads people to receive the now-fashionable descriptions as the truth.

Sexual desire, as it has been understood in every epoch prior to the present, is inherently compromising, and the choice to express it or to yield to it has been viewed as an existential choice, in which more is at risk than present satisfaction. Not surprisingly, therefore, the sexual act has been surrounded by prohibitions; it brings with it a weight of shame, guilt, and jealousy, as well as joy and happiness. Sex is therefore deeply implicated in the sense of original sin: the sense of being sundered from what we truly are, by our fall into the world of objects.

There is an important insight contained in the book of Genesis, concerning the place of shame in our understanding of sex. Adam and Eve have partaken of the forbidden fruit, and obtained the "knowledge of good and evil"—in other words the ability to invent for themselves the code that governs their behavior. God walks in the garden and they hide, conscious for the first time of their bodies as objects of shame. This "shame of the body" is an extraordinary feeling, and one that only a self-conscious animal could have. It is a recognition of the body as both intimately me and in some way not me—a thing that has wandered into the world of objects as though of its own accord, to become the victim of uninvited glances. Adam and Eve have become conscious that they are not only face-to-face, but joined in another way, as bodies, and, in Milton's incomparable version, the objectifying gaze of lust now poisons their once-innocent desire. By means of the fig leaf Adam and Eve are able to rescue each other from the worst: to ensure, however tentatively, that they can still be face-to-face, even if the erotic has now been privatized and attached to the private parts. In his well-known fresco of the expulsion from Paradise, Masaccio shows the distinction between the two shames—that of the body, which causes Eve to hide her sexual parts, and that of the soul, which causes Adam to hide his face. Adam hides the *self*; Eve shows the self in all its confused grief, but still protects the body—for that, she now knows, can be tainted by others' eyes (fig. 2).

The tree of knowledge that caused the fall of man is surely wrongly described as giving us the knowledge of good and evil. Rather, it gave us the knowledge of ourselves as objects—we fell from the realm

Fig. 2. Masaccio, *The Expulsion from Paradise*, Florence, Santa Maria del Carmine.
© 2013. Photo SCALA, Florence/Fondo Edifici di Culto—Min. dell'Interno.

of subjectivity into the world of things. We learned to look on each other as objects, and to sweep away the face and all that the face stands for. We lost what was most precious to us, which is the untorn veil of the *Lebenswelt*, stretching from horizon to horizon across the dark matter from which all things, we included, are composed.

The Myth of Origins

The story of man's fall is a "myth of origins." Such myths, which are a vital part of religion, display the layers of consciousness in *archaeological* terms, as though each layer is somehow "earlier" than the one that rests on it. In the religious frame of mind we read our nature "back to origins," in order to understand as a narrative what is in fact the truth about the present moment, in which we are forever trapped. The story of the Fall, as I have just recounted it, records a deep truth about the human psyche. It tells us that we are tempted to conceive our most intimate relations in objectifying terms, as an affair of bodies in which the other is no longer present as a subject in his face. But it represents this truth through a story of the "Fall," the particular transgression occurring at a particular moment, before which we enjoyed the purity that was thereafter lost to us. This story is a fiction, although a fiction that illustrates a truth.

All religions involve this kind of reversal, setting out the basic truths of self-conscious being in the form of a narrative of origins. The story of the creation is itself such a narrative—which is not to deny that the world is dependent upon God and an expression of his free creative power, but rather to insist that there is no "moment" of creation, no moment before which there was nothing, and after which time began to unfold. It is true that scientists trace our universe back to the "singularity" of the Big Bang, beyond which our understanding cannot venture, since the laws of physics operate only in the ensuing turmoil. But this does not imply that there was a moment of creation that sundered time into the period of nothingness and the something thereafter. Rather, it implies that we can give no content to the idea of empty time, in which case the narrative of creation, according to which God steps in to bring nothing to an end, is a story about nothing, and therefore not a story.

To describe a narrative as a "myth of origins" is not to reject it, but to say that it must be understood in another way, as a revelation of present realities. This is beautifully illustrated by Wagner in *The Ring of the Nibelung*, in which the narrative unfolds both forward and backward simultaneously. Each step that Wotan takes toward the resolution of his dilemmas uncovers some "earlier" measure that inexorably led to it, some deeper and more primeval encounter with the order of nature. The myth concerns an origin that lies so deeply buried that it can be understood only in retrospect, as the buried fragments are brought one by one into the light of consciousness. The meaning of these fragments is revealed in the "now." But this is an eternal "now": such is the burden of the mystical Prelude to *Götterdämmerung*, in which the Norns weave the rope of destiny, understanding their own actions only partially, and only in the thing that they produce. (The Rhine-daughters, themselves features of the eternal beginning, later describe the rope as the *Urgesetzes Seil*—the rope of the primeval, all-preceding law.) Wagner shows that the idealized freedom represented by Wotan—the freedom to command a world and to embellish it with law, security, and ownership—is a chimera, until realized in mortal flesh. But freedom is realized as love, and love demands renunciation. When Wotan understands this, he is ready to accept his own mortality. Wotan's spiritual journey began with his search for immortal glory; it ends with his conscious will toward death. Yet the "beginning" and the "end" are eternally present. Each contains the other: which is why the narrative unfolds as it does, in both directions at once.

The biblical narrative is very different, of course. Wagner was a dramatist and an anthropologist, who understood myths as myths, and presented them with all their paradoxes exposed. The biblical narrative, though clearly the product of a cunning intellect (or several cunning intellects, if the scholars are to be trusted), purports to be an account of what actually happened, in those six days of creation. It speaks of an original union of man and God, sundered by the free actions of our "first parents," after which mankind wandered the world in conflict and desolation. And the New Testament offers a final redemption, one already foretold by the prophets. The price of that original sin has now been paid by God himself, and the way back to oneness with God at last lies open before us.

That narrative exemplifies a pattern that is widely observed, not only in myths of origins, but also in rites of passage—in which individuals first separate from the tribe and then undergo a ritual reincorporation. We find it exemplified also in certain philosophical and poetic accounts of the nature and destiny of human societies.

The pattern is this: innocent unity, then guilty separation, leading at last to a recovered unity, in a state of understanding and forgiveness. In *The Mind of God and the Works of Man*, Edward Craig persuasively argues that the dominant philosophy of the romantic era in Germany derives from "the one great metaphysical theme with which the minds of this time were obsessed: unity, its loss and its recovery."[6] And he gives an account in these terms of "the great cosmic waltz, the metaphysical three-in-a-bar of Hegel's dialectic."[7] Yet it is not only the German romantics who saw the world in terms of this pervasive pattern. Many ancient religions have a comparable structure—notably the cults of Isis and Osiris, Attis, and Adonis. The Roman Catholic rite of confession, penitence, and absolution is likewise part of such a pattern, which is exemplified also in some of the Greek tragedies, notably in the *Oresteia* and in the extended narrative of Oedipus, ending in *Oedipus at Colonus*.

Still, Craig is right to pick on Hegel's dialectic, which is of additional interest on account of its quasi-temporal structure, consciously presenting logical presuppositions as though they were stages of a narrative, even using the word "moment" and the language of "earlier," "not yet," and "later" to lay out the inner structure of our mental life. It will help us to understand the significance of the face, and of human subjectivity as revealed in the face, if we pause to consider what Hegel had in mind.

Hegel, the Dialectic, and Self-Consciousness

The dialectic, according to Hegel, is a structure that we uncover in all the practices that have freedom, consciousness, or knowledge as their goal. Such practices "begin" from a moment of immersion, in which the subject has a consciousness that is "immediate" and "abstract." The subject proceeds toward concrete knowledge only by a movement outward, toward that which "limits" and "determines" the

<hr>

[6]Edward Craig, *The Mind of God and the Works of Man* (Oxford: Clarendon Press, 1987), p. 136.

[7]Ibid., p. 151.

boundaries of the self. The subject experiences this limiting factor as something *other*, a genuine *object* of knowledge, and not simply an aspect of the self. The outward movement, or *Entäusserung*, introduces the crucial moment of alienation or estrangement. The search for knowledge engenders conflict, without which there can be no recognition of an objective world, or of the subject's own place within that world. The conflict is then overcome, transcended into a new level of freedom, from which the dialectical process can begin again. The entire trajectory of conscious life can be, indeed must be, described in these terms, as successive movements from the abstract and immediate to the concrete and determinate, proceeding through conflict to the moment of transcendence when opposition is overcome and reconciled. In this picture, the pattern of innocent unity, followed by guilty separation, followed by reconciliation in a state of knowledge, is presented as the fundamental structure of consciousness.

If we see the Hegelian dialectic as a "myth of origins," all that takes on a new aspect. We then understand the tripartite division of conscious life as a permanent structure in consciousness itself. It is not that the things described as "moments" or "stages" succeed each other in time, but that they lie, as it were, enfolded in the psyche in a relation of mutual dependence. This can be illustrated by reflecting on the two aspects of our being that Kant singled out for special attention: self-consciousness (which he called "apperception") and freedom.

Self-consciousness begins, according to the dialectical narrative, in the immediate ("criterionless") awareness of a unified world, in which the inner and the outer are not yet distinguished. But awareness demands an object, and the object of awareness, once "posited,"[8] lies outside the self and also conflicts with it by presenting a boundary and a limit to subjective desires. Objects are "to be used." They thwart my desires and can also fulfill them. Through my interaction with objects I encounter the other, who conflicts with me for their possession and use. Through the long struggle that follows, which has as many "moments" as there are layers of self-consciousness, the subject comes

---

[8] The verb is *setzen*, introduced in this connection by Fichte to denote the original creative power of subjectivity. See the *Wissenschaftslehre* (1794).

to recognize that he too is other to those who conflict with him. His knowledge of himself is now "mediated" by a concept of the objective world, in which he is situated as one self-conscious agent among others. And this recognition opens the way back from alienation—or rather the way forward to a new kind of unity. This unity is not the unity of the self with itself, the empty self-identity from which the process began, but a unity of self and other, a reconciliation in the mutual dealings of subjects who acknowledge each other as free. It is at this point that the moral life, the life in society, begins.

That narrative should be rewritten in "logical" form, with presupposition rather than succession as the guiding relation. The resulting picture is this: I exist as a subject, that is, as a self-conscious being with immediate knowledge of an inner realm, which defines my point of view on the world. But this presupposes that I exist in a world of objects to which I can refer and which I can identify as other than myself. Reference in turn presupposes others, with whom I share language and therefore the first-person perspective. And language presupposes a shared world, a *Lebenswelt*, in which others are represented as subjects like myself. In sum, self-consciousness presupposes all those "later" stages of alienation from, and reconciliation with, the other, as these are described in Hegel's narrative.

Freedom

Likewise the story of freedom can be written in two ways. According to the "myth of origins" version, the free subject begins with an original freedom, which is immediate and "indeterminate." This freedom is, as Hegel puts it, the *"bei sich selbst"* of the I: mere self-sufficiency.[9] Freedom can become real and determinate only if exercised in a world that is *other than*, *outside* the subjectivity of the agent. Until realized in an objective world, freedom is a dream, not an exercise of rational choice, nor a form of self-determination and self-knowledge. But the subject, exercising his freedom in the world of objects, enters into conflict with others who are doing the same. In this conflict

[9] *Lectures on the Philosophy of History*, Introduction B (a).

each regards the other as an obstacle, an object to be subdued. In other words, subjects begin by treating each other as objects. Being objects for each other, each becomes an object to himself, entering the state of alienation in which the value of freedom is as though veiled by need and appetite. The alienated world is one in which the agent finds no worth in his own being, and no reason for his actions, which are compelled from him by the pressure of events. Only when the parties recognize each other as free subjects do they come to act from reasons. For reasons are public, valid for all rational agents, and phrased in terms of the world that they share—the *Lebenswelt*. Practical reasons are rooted in the recognition that free agents accord to each other, when they come to accept each other as ends in themselves. In other words, freedom is fully realized only in the world of persons, bound together by rights and duties that are mutually recognized. It is then concrete, determinate freedom, through which agents achieve the full consciousness of themselves and of their reasons for doing what they do.

Of course, those are not Hegel's words, and my story condenses many hundreds of pages into a single paragraph. But it suffices to show that the "myth of origins" narrative stands proxy for another, in which presupposition again replaces succession as the binding relation between the "moments." The freedom of the subject presupposes membership of a world in which the distinction can be drawn between the ends of action and the means needed to secure them. That distinction is made available by practical reason, which in turn presupposes a community of rational beings who respect each other as persons and recognize in each other the freedom that is realized through their deals and projects. In short, the immediate knowledge of my own freedom, which is the premise of practical reason, also presupposes the world that practical reason creates, the shared *Lebenswelt*, structured by deontic powers.

The "myth of origins" approach to self-consciousness and freedom enables us to perceive the complexity of these two aspects of our condition. Each can be unfolded into the layers that compose it, and each layer tells us something more about the *Lebenswelt*. The face is illuminated as though from within by self-consciousness and freedom, and each face that we encounter looks at us from outside the natural order. The face is not an object among objects, and when people invite us to perceive it as such, in the manner of pornography, they succeed only in defacing the human form. In describing the role of the face in interpersonal relations, I have been trying to illustrate an important truth about the *Lebenswelt*, and a crucial axiom of my kind of cognitive dualism. This is the truth that surfaces are deep. Enfolded within the glance, the blush, the kiss, and the smile are those layers of being that are more easily set out in Hegel's way, through a myth of origins, than in the way familiar to analytical philosophers. The subject is revealed in his face as free, self-conscious, self-knowing, and he acquires these characteristics in part because they are realized, made public, in his face. By coming face-to-face with others, we gain full awareness of the constraints of practical reason, and therefore of the freedom that our social membership bestows on us.

When Sellars introduced his distinction between the manifest and the scientific image, he argued, in a way not entirely remote from my thoughts in this chapter, that the idea of the person is central to the manifest image, and that with the idea of the person comes that of the community. The manifest image represents a shared cognitive investment. Nevertheless Sellars hoped to establish the "primacy of the scientific image," and he regarded that thesis as fundamental to the new philosophical task. He believed that the "manifest image" is somehow shallow, the effect of what Hume called the "mind's capacity to spread itself upon objects," something to be *peeled away*, so as to reveal the truth of the world, which is the story told by science. (Thus, according to one traditional empiricist account, science strips the world of secondary qualities, which are merely the colors that the world wears from our perspective, and describes it in terms of primary qualities alone.) But when we look at the example of the face, we see that this picture is profoundly misleading. The manifest image is full, rich, and deep. The most important aspects of the human condition are to be discovered in its folds, sequestered there like harmonies in music and the stories shown in pictures, telling us what we really and deeply are. The face, for us, is the real presence of a person; it is the image of freedom, shaped by the demands of social life.

To say what it is we see when we see a face, a smile, a look, we must use concepts from another language than the language of science, and make connections of another kind from those that are the subject matter of causal laws. And what we witness, when we see the world in this way, is something far more important to us, and far more replete with meaning, than anything that could be captured by the biological sciences. Through the example of the face we understand a little of what Oscar Wilde meant, when he said that it is only a very shallow person who does not judge by appearances.

6

Facing the Earth

Myths of origins are not ordinary fairy tales or explorations of the supernatural. They are attempts to make sense of the human condition, by projecting human nature back to an imaginary origin unencumbered by history and institutions. The myth displays a world in which persons exist *from the beginning*, and uses that device to explore the predicament of persons here and now. Rousseau's story of the "noble savage" is such a myth; so too is the "social contract" theory of the state. And because it is in the nature of persons to flourish only in a state of mutual recognition and reciprocal accountability, personhood involves the search for righteousness and the possibility of guilt. In the story of the Fall this deep truth about the human condition is transcribed as a myth of origins. Of such a myth it should not be said that it is simply a story, empty of truth. On the contrary, it is a truth, concealed within a story. In this chapter I will try to say more about that truth, in the context of another story.

Myths of origins contrast sharply with the science of origins, as this has developed in the wake of Darwin. It is the fashion to explain emotionally charged features of personal life as "adaptations," meaning responses selected in "our environment of evolutionary adaptedness." Many of our mostly deeply implanted traits, it is argued, came about during the years of the hunter-gatherer community. That community had the benefit of language and tools, but not the benefit of law, religion, or agriculture, which arose in later times, when humans began to settle and cultivate the land. For the evolutionary psychologist human nature is largely composed of these deep adaptations, and they are best understood as solutions to the problems of survival, in circumstances that have now largely disappeared.

One reason why civilizations have so often treated human nature as an obstacle, and have fought against it with all the weapons that law, religion, and morality could provide, is that we address the world from a genetic inheritance that we have in a certain way surpassed. The impulses to destroy the intruder, to cast out the critic, to submit to the powerful leader, and to kill, enslave, or violate the captive are no doubt adaptive in the harsh conditions in which tribes compete for scarce resources among wild beasts and natural disasters. But they disrupt the work of civilization and must be channeled in other directions or even suppressed entirely if we are to flourish as persons flourish, in a condition of reciprocal accountability.[1] The science of origins traces our psychology to impulses that are only doubtfully interpersonal, and which have to be overcome precisely in order that we should flourish as free subjects, and not as animals enslaved by our genes.

How then do we explain the transition from the life of the human animal to that of the human person? We know that the transition occurred. And we surmise that it occurred gradually, as old adaptations yielded to the pressure of social reciprocity. But the end result—the emergence of free subjects, bound by rights and duties to others of their kind—is a condition that cannot be understood through the laws of biology. This condition emerged from the natural order, but is not a part of it. That is why, when we try to imagine how it is that people have become what they are, we so often have recourse to a "myth of origins." We tell a story in which we appear from the outset as the "everlasting man," in Chesterton's phrase—the thing that we in fact become only over time and, in a certain measure, inexplicably.[2] Religions help us to understand ourselves by providing myths of that kind.

Not that these myths are without foundation. Often they can be rewritten in a more analytical idiom, in the way that Hegel's dialectic can be rewritten in terms of the presupposition rather than succession between its "moments." Moreover, there is another idea of Hegel's, explicit already in Aristotle, which gives purchase to the narrative conception of the *Lebenswelt*. Aristotle wrote of the potency (*dunamis*) of an entity, and the full expansion of that potency in its activity (*energeia*) or in its fulfilled and completed form (*entelechia*). Medieval writers, following Aristotle, distinguished the potential of

[1] I develop this argument at greater length in *The Uses of Pessimism and the Danger of False Hope* (London: Atlantic Books, 2010; New York, Oxford University Press, 2011).
[2] G. K. Chesterton, *The Everlasting Man* (San Francisco: Ignatius Press, 1993).

a thing from the act that realizes it. Put very simply, there are entities whose essence consists in the power to develop in a certain way.
What such entities essentially are can often be fully comprehended
only in terms of their final form. It is of the essence of an acorn that
it will (unless impeded by some defect or disease) grow into an oak.
And we understand what an acorn *is* only by understanding what it
becomes. Likewise, while there are human beings who do not exhibit
the defining traits of personality, human beings are nevertheless essentially persons, since it is in their nature to become persons and to
be fulfilled as persons. Personhood is the *telos*, the end, of each of us.

Hegel argued that it is in the nature of consciousness to strive for
"realization," or "objectification" (*Entäusserung*) so as to attain determinate and objective form. The story told by the dialectic can be
understood in another, and atemporal, way, as defining what has to
occur for a thing to be fully realized. Thus people have their freedom abstractly and unconditionally; but what this freedom truly is
can be understood only in terms of its objective realization in the
institutions of the state. The state is contained in the seed of freedom as the oak tree in the acorn. The narrative of *The Philosophy of
Right* tells us about the layers of reflective consciousness that are realized in political institutions. And it is often helpful, when trying to
understand the mutual dependence that binds these layers together,
to provide a narrative that builds by stages toward the reality that
is secretly presupposed from the outset. This narrative will have no
relation to the story told by the evolutionary psychologist. For its pro-
tagonists throughout are persons, subjects of reflective consciousness,
and therefore already by-products of an evolutionary process that lies
in the hidden background. The evolutionary story describes the machinery behind the backdrop that, even if revealed, would have no
intelligible relation to the action on the stage.

Settlement and the City

Just such a myth of origins is called for in describing the relation
of persons to the places where they dwell. Not every habitat is fit
for persons, and the paradigm that history presents to us is, from
the biological point of view, an anomaly. All that we know of the

life that defines us we know from the history, art, and literature of
settled peoples, who have cleared the land of competing forms of
life, planted crops, and raised in the midst of their fields the city, as a
refuge for themselves and for their gods. The story that they tell is our
story, and it tells us how we might dwell in the places that we have
taken into possession.

In the religion of the ancient Greeks and Romans the hearth, and
the fire that glows in it, have a special significance, as representing the
will to settle of the family whose land lies round about. It is here that
room is made for the household gods, and it is here that members of
the family gather for the ritual acknowledgment of the ancestors who
established their title to be where they are. Archaeologists and anthropologists do not have a single opinion about the origins of the associated religious beliefs, though it is clear that the Greeks, the Romans,
and the Etruscans worshipped gods whose forms and powers were
also known in ancient India. The Sanskrit word for god—*deva*—is
recalled in Latin *deus* and Greek *theos*, as are some of the names of the
divine personalities, notably Jupiter, the sky god, who is *Dyauspitr* in
the Vedas.[3] The Vedas make much of *Agni*, the god of fire (Latin *ignus*),
who sanctifies the hearth, and protects it as the sovereign sphere of the
family that eats, prays, and rests in its vicinity.

The cult of the hearth went hand in hand with the worship of ancestors, whose presence is acknowledged in the rituals of the household and in the gods (the *lares et penates*) who have been handed
down as a family possession. When people are settled in a place, they
experience a dominant metaphysical need—the need for the authoritative proof that this place is *ours*, that we are entitled to it and can
call upon the law of the universe to protect our right to it. Ancestor worship helps to supply this need. The dead that lie beneath the
hearth or entombed beside it respond to our prayers, and their spiritual presence confirms our ownership, which is exercised not on our
behalf only but also on theirs. The regime of property, so fundamental to the building of cities and the settlement of the land, arises then
as a religious imperative.

---

[3] An archaic form of the Latin name is Diespiter, "Day Father," occurring in poetic usage
(e.g., Horace, *Odes* 1.34).

Those unsurprising observations open the way to understanding another myth of origins and another manifestation of "original sin." In *La Cité antique*, published in 1864, the historian Fustel de Coulanges tells the story of the ancient city, which he sees primarily as a religious foundation, one in which people assemble to protect their households, their ancestors, and their gods, and in which each family gains an enduring foothold. Religion and family grow together, as a single and eternal imperative; and from their union is born the household, the regime of property, and the sacred sphere of domestic life. The religion of the ancients was in this way adapted to their agrarian way of life, and to the small spheres of local sovereignty through which they exerted their hold on the land.

Little by little, according to the story told by Fustel de Coulanges, the families combined into large associations, genera, tribes, phratries, as we know them from the laws of the city-states of Greece and Rome. And at a certain point there emerged the idea of the City, as a political association, and of the town as its physical embodiment. The foundation of the city was made possible only by radical changes in the worship of those who were to be its citizens. In addition to the family gods, who survived in their spheres of private sovereignty, new and more public gods emerged, with the function of uniting people from several families in shared forms of worship and a shared loyalty to the common soil. In the story of the foundation of Rome we find an archetype of the transition from worship of the hearth, and of the ancestors whom it had engendered, to the public ceremonies devoted to the gods of the city—gods to which no family had an exclusive claim. Every ancient town was founded by an act of consecration, and built around the altars of its protecting gods. In the words of Fustel, "*toute ville était un sanctuaire; toute ville pouvait être appelée sainte.*"

In the eyes of the citizens the city was a gift bestowed upon them by the gods, who protected the residents and authenticated their laws. In the scriptures of the Israelites the city acquires another kind of myth of origins. God's gift of laws and covenants is intended to guide his people in the way of the Lord. But law in the Hebrew Bible does not stand alone, nor are God's commandments offered as though arbitrary, and without foundation in the personal relations that God upholds and claims. On the contrary, the law is connected from the outset with the concept of neighbor love, the love that Saint Paul calls *agape* and which (to use Kant's idiom) is commanded as a law. The life among neighbors is what God is regulating through the Ten Commandments—a life that transcends the boundaries of family, and which strays into territory that the ancestors cannot easily invigilate. And God adds another commandment to the Ten, namely, that the Israelites should build a home for him—a temple in which the architecture and the rituals will invite the real presence of the Lord.

The Temple

It is natural to believe that places are made sacred by the temple that is built on them, and by the act of consecration that initiates the building: such is implied in the Greek and Roman myths. In the Old Testament, however, it is the other way round. The patriarchs erect altars, make sacrifices, bestow names on places rendered holy by some encounter with God and his angels. Nor should this surprise us. The idea of the sacred place seems to be a human universal, and it is only the special circumstances of the agrarian people of the Mediterranean that made the hearth into the paradigm of a consecrated space. For some cultures gods, spirits, and other supernatural agents live among us, and must be worshipped or acknowledged at the spot where they reside. For others a place becomes sacred because it is the haunt of a ghost, maybe the ghost of someone who has died with some deep need unsatisfied or some deep love denied, and whose moment of crisis occurred at this very spot: this idea you find in the Shinto religion, and dramatized in the Noh theater of Japan. Sorrows *inhabit* the world, and haunt the places where they were suffered.

Other cultures connect sacred places with the legends of heroes or with great battles of the past, to which we come to pay respects for some patriotic sacrifice. In all societies in which dead people are ceremonially buried, the place of burial becomes "hallowed ground," and ritualized acts and words are deemed appropriate when we walk there. Funerary rites, beliefs about the gods and the afterlife, invocations of ancestors, and declarations of solidarity with the dead and the unborn—these are the core experiences from which lasting cultures derive, and they find expression in graveyards and tombs at every age and in every place.

The Jewish patriarchs regarded the Promised Land not as a thing to consume and discard but as an inheritance, to be cared for and passed on. This was how they justified the cruel, and in modern eyes unforgivable, extermination of the Canaanites, as recounted in the book of Joshua. And this feeling was bound up with two others: their conviction that God was a real presence among them, and their sense of the land as a gift—not a gift to the present generation to use as it will, but a gift to a people in its entirety and for all time, a resource to be renewed and passed on. This records a general truth about the sacred. Sacred places are protected from spoliation; they are steeped in the hopes and the sufferings of those who have fought for them. And they belong to others who are yet to be.

Such a sentiment tied the Israelites to the Promised Land, and to the Holy City that was built in it. God had presented Moses with the design for a sanctuary (Exod. 25:8), and it is around this temple that the city of Jerusalem was built—the shining city on the hill that is the sacred place to which God's people turn from their tribulations. By the time of the Psalms the sanctity of the temple and that of the city have become one—for the true settlement is one in which God dwells among us, and its destruction is an act of sacrilege that changes the face of the world.

> *If I forget thee, O Jerusalem,*
> > *Let my right hand forget her cunning.*
> *If I do not remember thee*
> > *Let my tongue cleave to the roof of my mouth;*
> *If I prefer not Jerusalem above my chief joy.*

The spoiling of the earth and the vandalizing of our human habitats arouse in us an echo of the desolation that the psalmist records in those words: the desolation that ensues when a place loses its *spiritus loci*, is reduced to ruins, and ceases to be a home within the *Lebenswelt*. And it seems to me that we will not understand what is really at stake in the environmental consciousness that has captured the imagination of so many people today, if we do not recognize a religious memory at the heart of it.

God's message concerning the temple was not simply the foundation of a specific cult, devoted to the god of a tribe. It was a message
to all of us, telling us that God will dwell among us only if we too
dwell, and that dwelling does not mean consuming the earth or wast-
ing it, but conserving it, so as to make a lasting sanctuary for both
God and man. Hence the promise of God's kingdom in the book of
Revelation is a promise of the "New Jerusalem," the Holy City, in
which we live side by side with each other and face-to-face with God.
The theme of the Holy City, which is the measure and ideal of all our
settlements, was made central to Christian life by Saint Augustine,
in *The City of God*. We might summarize the message concerning
the ancient temple, in its pagan as much as its Judeo-Christian version, thus: a true city begins from an act of consecration, and it is the
temple that is the model for all other dwellings.

Another Myth of Origins

That story is also a myth of origins. This myth does not tell of our
expulsion from Paradise and our separation from God. Rather it tells
of our rescue from wandering and conflict by the collective decision
to dwell, so as once again to be united, though in another way, with
the God who had expelled us from our former dwelling place. The
story begins with a temple, and that temple must be fit for the god
who inhabits it. It must be a permanent home, expressing an eternal
presence in the city. Hence the founding temple of the city should
be of stone. It should contain a sanctuary, in which the god can be
both concealed from his worshippers and revealed to his priests. But
it must also be a public place. The temple symbolizes the collective
intention to dwell in this place where the community has made a renewed bid for permanence. Hence it should be permeable to the city,
perhaps surrounded by an open space, and with colonnades, aisles,
cloisters, precincts in which citizens can freely associate in the benign
presence of the god who watches over them.

At the same time, the temple is not fully a part of the city. Metaphysically speaking, it is a place on the city's edge, the place that is
filled by the god. Its architecture must show this—it must point away

from this world, as well as being open to the world's transactions. The "reference beyond" of sacred architecture reflects the overreaching intentionality of our interpersonal attitudes. The I of God resides in this place, and architecture makes us aware of that. It is not simply stone that surrounds us, but a *witnessing* stone, stone brought alive by carving, molding, light and shade, so as to stand beside us in an observing posture. The temple is the place where the faithful can encounter God. But he is also hidden there, concealed in the inner sanctum, or in rituals that only the few can decipher. The temple reveals God by concealing him, and this paradox is symbolized in its structure and form. Churches, mosques, and temples still convey this feeling, even to the one who enters them in unbelief. They are places haunted by an "invisible presence," and their forms and details have the look of things that are looked at by unseen eyes.

The source of this feeling in the human psyche is touched on by Saint Paul, in the first letter to the Corinthians (6:19): "Do you not know that your body is a temple of the Holy Spirit, who is in you, whom you have received from God?" The human body is the place where the other is both present and hidden, protected from me but nevertheless revealed when the right words are uttered and the right gestures made. "There is but one temple in the world," wrote Novalis (*Hymns to the Night*), "and that is the body of man . . . We touch Heaven when we lay our hand on a human body." In everyday life we don't see things in quite that way. But in the intimacy of love, anger, or desire I encounter the other as *haunted by himself.* I look *into* him, and he becomes a presence that I sense but which flees from my attempts to conjure it, until the right look or word or touch brings it suddenly to rest and face-to-face with me. It is on this experience that we draw, when we respond to the temple as a shrine. God is a real presence in his temple, as you are in your body.

The parallel between the body and the temple influences the forms of sacred architecture. Like the human being, the temple stands upright. It is not a single monolith any more than the human body is a continuous solid. It is the exfoliation of a generative code, contained within the primary unit of the column, the dimensions of which provide the scalar measure for the entire building. This we learn from the study of the classical Orders, but not only from them, as Otto von Simson showed in his great book on the Gothic cathedral.[4] The generative nature of temple architecture is a *spiritualizing* feature of it. Everywhere the stone bears the mark of a shaping intention. Elements are fitted together in the relationship that Alberti described as *concinnitas*—which means the apt correspondence of part to part, the ability of one detail to give a clear visual answer to the "why?" posed by another.[5] A temple is not simply a work of load-bearing stone. The column is carved, fluted, adorned with plinth and capital, crowned by a frieze or an arch, or joined in heavenly vaults where stone achieves the lightness of the sky. Through moldings and decorative details the stone is filled with shadow, acquires a translucent appearance, as the face is translucent to the spirit within.

Colophon Imagined

I quote here from a work of my own, a sequel to *Xanthippic Dialogues* entitled *Perictione in Colophon*. The book tells the story of Archeanassa, identified (absurdly) by Diogenes Laertius as the mistress of Plato,[6] who finds herself in her native city of Colophon, entertained there by Plato's niece Perictione, a dancer in a high-class nightclub. The city, now occupied by the Persians, has been obliterated by highrise towers devoted to the inscrutable bureaucracy that has replaced the free life of the Greek *polis*, and Perictione, exasperated by Archeanassa's complaints against this development, asks her to explain how

---

[4]Otto von Simson, *The Gothic Cathedral* (London: Routledge, 1956).
[5]*De re aedificatoria* (1452), trans. Leoni, 1726.
[6]Diogenes Laertius, in his lives of the philosophers, attributes to Plato a poem, now thought to be a funerary inscription, which I translate freely as follows:

Archeanassa is my girl, she of Colophon,
Upon whose very wrinkles sits desire;
You bastards, you who boarded her upon
Her maiden trip, I bet she stoked your fire!

This outburst of obsessive sexual jealousy on Plato's part is explained in *Phryne's Symposium*, the last of *Xanthippic Dialogues*, ed. Roger Scruton (London: Sinclair-Stevenson, 1992). *Perictione in Colophon* is published by St. Augustine's Press (Chicago, 2001), as is *Xanthippic Dialogues*.

the old city of Colophon was built. She responds with the following myth of origins.

"On this hill, rising from a valley of orchards and pastures, with simple cottages of limestone, and neatly laid walls and terraces of the same material, the founders of Colophon built a temple to Artemis, and placed themselves under the goddess's protection, dedicating festivals to her honor and teaching the Artemisian dances to their children. The temple was of stone, with Ionic columns, for such was the style in Lydia. It was not large, but so perfect were its proportions that the Colophonians forbade all building next to it, and laid out a garden, with trees of lime wood and hornbeam, to serve as a temple precinct. And it was from the dialogue between the temple and its garden that the city grew. Some brought gifts of furniture and statuary to the temple; others embellished the garden with shrubs and lawns and fountains. And each addition to the temple found some answering ornament outside, until the precinct became as much a work of architecture as if it had been built of stone instead of grass and wood and growing things.

"Now there is much to be learned from gardens, and especially from gardens of the kind that I am describing. In such places the plants, buildings, and furniture have no special use. There is a purpose to the farmer's fields and the merchant's storehouse, but not to the lawns and statues in a garden. Each object is there for no purpose but itself. And we too, when we visit the precinct, leave our purposes behind. We wander in the shade, refresh our spirits with the sight of clear water sparkling over amber stones, and listen to the birds as they sing above us. And all for no purpose other than our delight in these things. Moreover, the garden is a social place. People cross each other's path, fall into conversation, perhaps play games together or sit side by side at peace. And these ways of being in a garden are of peculiar significance, Perictione; for they too are free from purpose. People in a garden are *beyond* purpose, in a side-by-sideness that is also an alertness to the world . . .

"There, in our municipal garden, we were at peace with each other and the world. And it is from peace that the city was built. Here is a curious fact. The column of a temple has often been compared to the trunk of a tree . . . [But] the comparison is in one sense highly misleading. The tree trunk is far higher than the column; it is covered in blemishes and irregularities, spreads into branches of every shape and size, culminates in no capital, and rises from the ground directly and without a base. In short, it is unlike the column in every respect, save for the fact that it stands to attention—and even then, it does so only in gardens and parks. Why then do people dwell so much on this comparison? The important point, it seems to me, is the play of light and shade. The spangled sunbeams pierce the canopy of leaves, one thing casts its shade over another, and to each object that stands is given a shadow lying beside it. Shadow is the language of standing things, the medium of their dialogue. And the trunk of the tree is the place of shadows, through which it reaches to the light . . .

"Like the tree trunk, the column stands before us. And like the trunk, it is a place of light and shade. It begins from a base, around which concave moldings form a belt of darkness. It rises with a single gesture to the capital, where it flowers into carved volutes, with all kinds of delicate bands and ribs and flutings that I lack the language to describe, but which are in any case more familiar to the eye than any words can make them. Sometimes, to enhance the effect, the architect will add flutes to the shaft, so that the column is transformed into long blades of golden light, laid on the fluffy shadow. And if you were to compare this fluting to the bark of a tree, which is the great gatherer and enfolder of shadows and the means whereby the tree steals the light surrounding it, you would again be in error. For the bark of a tree is an outgrowth, its edges are relinquishings, and its shadows lie as do the shadows on a hillside, in valleys and crevasses among slopes that swell and rise. The fluting of a column, however, is an incision, something carved by exploring hands, a hollowing out and sculpting of the stone. Its edges are honed: they probe and question the air, and the light is not stolen by the channel but lives in it, like a smile in a face. And if I were to say what a column is essentially, what it is when judged in terms of its real meaning to the one who stands in its vicinity, I should not say that it is stone, or marble or wood. I should say that it is crystallized light. And by capturing light in this way, we Greeks educated ourselves in the use of it. The temple became the model for all other building, and rightly so, since by following this model we merely extend and furnish our common home.

" . . . You notice, I am sure, that the towers of modern Colophon have no orientation, no privileged approach, no gestures or expressions that conduct you into their vicinity. They face nothing, welcome nothing, smile and nod to no one. Hence we cannot stand comfortably in their presence.

"Nor is that all. The modern tower, which ignorant people might compare to the temple column, is in reality the very opposite. For the modern tower lacks everything that gives meaning to the column. It has neither base nor capital; it avoids moldings, stringcourses, and ornaments as though they were crimes, and its surface is devoid of significant shadow and therefore devoid of light—for light needs shade if it is to be seen. The tower escapes upward as though fleeing from itself; but it concludes in nothing—neither entablature nor pitched roof cushion the sky, which it wounds with blunt aggressive punches . . .

"And for those very reasons, although the tower is tall, vertical, and slim, it does not really stand before us. For it has no posture and no repose. Its vertical extent expresses no vertical order. On the contrary, its order is horizontal. The tower is composed as a ground-plan, which is then projected upward through slab upon slab and floor upon floor, until the required number of desks or beds or cells can be accommodated. To make the design easy to execute, the plan is regular—usually square or oblong. And this means that the tower must be constructed in a cleared site, and rises up surrounded by empty lots and destroyed streets.

The Street and the Pattern Book

"And perhaps this is what I most dislike in this Colophon of yours— that it has no streets. Oh, I grant you, there are thoroughfares and boulevards, carved through the city like swathes through a field of corn. But these thoroughfares are not lined by houses standing side by side and leaning against each other. They are not overseen by dwellings, and their borders are not thresholds between public and private space. Nothing stands along them in a posture of repose, and even the air above them is lashed and torn by wires.

"To my way of thinking a true street is like a garden—not a means but an end. It is a place where you linger and take stock; where you meet and converse; where you stand beside objects that stand beside you. The new thoroughfare is not an end but a means: it is a conduit from one place to another. The buildings that occur along its edges are merely dumped there, offending both earth and sky by their inability to connect to either.

"No sooner did houses arise in ancient Colophon, than streets arose along with them. For those old houses stood side by side, facing in the same direction. And people stood at the gates conversing. Soon, in front of each row of houses, a public space came into being, a space that was every bit as consecrated as the garden beside the temple. The citizens, in order to express their pride in the city, and to mark out the land not as mine or yours or his, but as ours, began to provide this public space with furnishings. They paved it with cobbles, lined it on each side with flagstones of polished slate, and erected little shrines of porphyry or marble, in order that the gods should be at home there, which was the home of everyone. Those streets stitched the town together, and provided arteries through which its life could flow. And so pleased were the Colophonians with their appearance that they discussed in the assembly how best to conserve them, and how to ensure that this public space should remain always ours, and never his or hers.

"After much deliberation, they passed a law, which decreed that in future all houses and shops and workplaces built in Colophon must face onto a street, and that no building should be higher than those first houses by the garden of Artemis, save the temples of the gods, the assembly rooms, and the public library, which was to be the symbol of their civic pride and through which they declared that what mattered most to them after the gods was the idea of Greece. And they decreed that whatever was built in Colophon, be it house or shop or temple, must be built in stone, and in a style set out in the Colophonian pattern book . . .

"The pattern book did not forbid innovation, but controlled it, on the assumption that the pathbreaking gestures in architecture had already occurred, and that the city required a work of consolidation. Architecture cannot progress as music and poetry progress, so as to conform solely to the needs of genius. Architecture is a public enterprise: the architect does not build for the private client, but for the city. All of us are compelled to live with the result, which must therefore be offensive to no one. Originality should be second to good manners. The case is no different from clothing, which ought to be original only if it first conforms. The pattern book resulted from a long process of trial and error, whereby the appearance of the city and the feelings of the citizen were gradually brought into harmony and an easy conversational relation established between buildings and their passersby . . .

"But I have not identified the real difference between ancient and modern Colophon, or the real way in which we shape and are shaped by our buildings. These things cannot be understood, it seems to me, in secular terms. Our architecture derives from the temple, for the reason that the city derives from its god. The stone of the temple is the earthly translation of the god's immortality, which is in turn the symbol of a community and its will to live. The temple, like the liturgy, is forever, and the community contains not the living only, but also the dead and the unborn. And the dead are protected by the temple, which immortalizes them in stone. This is what you understand instinctively, when you see religious architecture. And it is the sentiment from which cities grow—the tribe's will to permanence . . .

" . . . From the permeable temple came the colonnade and thence the column, as the unit of meaning and the principle of our architectural grammar. In ancient Colophon the buildings conformed to this grammar, but with such variety and humor as befits the members of a peaceful crowd. And in each of them, sensed but not seen, was a column, standing immovably as the spirit stands immovably and invisibly in each of us. The column was permanent in the midst of change, and endorsed our sense of belonging. In our streets and temples and garden, therefore, we Colophonians perceived a visible license to dwell, an affirmation of our right of occupation, and a reminder that we belonged to a community that included our ancestors and progeny as well as ourselves. The civility of our buildings was a matter of manners and decency—for these are the virtues of the citizen, of the one who has settled in the land and renounced the habits of those nomads who take what they can from the earth and move on, leaving their waste behind.

"And then the Persians came, driving new hordes of nomads before them. A new architecture arose, and with it a new form of human life. These unarticulated verticals and blank screens of wall, these flattened deserts that once were streets, with the empty lots still grieving for their vanished houses—all speak of a flight from the city into some distant barricaded place, where neighborliness expires and people live for themselves alone. Vast and overbearing though the buildings of new Colophon may be, they have no air of permanence. The town is like a frozen junkyard, and even if it looks like this forever, it will look forever temporary. The raw utility of these buildings speaks not of us and our right of dwelling, but of *them*, the anonymous powers that are using us, for inscrutable purposes of their own. That is why these buildings are perceived as a desecration: nothing of the sacred remains in them . . ."

The Fallen World

Archeanassa's complaints against modern architecture derive from a myth of origins that places the consecrated temple at the heart of the city: the temple is the place of God's gaze. It has this character through standing and conversing, through inhabiting its space as a sphere of freedom, and through repulsing the officious demands of mere utility, announcing its existence as an end in itself. By contrast the new forms of architecture make no reference to the sacred origins of the city, and treat buildings as instruments, in something like the way that we have treated human beings as instruments. And surely it is not unrealistic to connect the two developments. We have fallen into the habit of seeing everything, ourselves included, as a thing to be used and exploited, and this is what our fall consists in. My discussion in the previous chapter connected this habit with "the ethic of pollution and taboo," as the anthropologists used to describe it. There is, in human affairs, a primordial temptation, which is the temptation to treat persons as things, and the embodied soul as a body. This habit of "defacing" the other might well be an adaptation from the evolutionary point of view; but, from the point of view of religion, it is also a desecration. As I argued in the previous chapter, the temptation to look on others as objects is what we mean or ought to mean by original sin. Here is what I there wrote:

> The tree of knowledge that caused the fall of man . . . gave us the knowledge of ourselves as objects—we fell from the realm of subjectivity into the world of things. We learned to look on each other as objects, and to sweep away the face and all that the face stands for. We lost what was most precious to us, which is the untorn veil of the *Lebenswelt,* stretching from horizon to horizon across the dark matter from which all things, we included, are composed.

When we see the world exclusively as an assemblage of objects, then nothing is rescued from barter and exchange. That is what we now do to each other and to the earth. It is also what we do to our habitat, which is ceasing to be a home and becoming instead a "machine for living in," as Le Corbusier, the ideologist of modernist planning, described his ideal house. To return to Archeanassa's myth: we made a second home for ourselves after the Fall, and that home was the City, the consecrated place where law, civility, and manners brought a kind of peace—not the peace that passeth understanding, which we left behind in Paradise, but peace as a shared possession, tainted by mortality, but the best that we mortals can do. And now, destroying that home, we are making a new kind of fallen world.

To the Greek city we owe our ideals of government and free inquiry. To the Romans we owe the gift of territorial law, and of the city shaped by law. But politics and law are not the ground on which the city rests. That ground, Archeanassa says, is religious. And she upholds, in her own way, the myth put before us by Fustel de Coulanges. The Roman building types—arch, aedicule, engaged column, pilaster, vault, and dome—can all be seen as attempts to retain the sacred presence of the column, in the uses of civic life. In them we see the interpenetration of the sacred and the secular, and thus the sanctifying of the human community and the humanizing of the divine. That is the source of their appeal and the reason for their durability. With the Roman building types began the true history of Western architecture: which is the history of the *implied Order.* This

Fig. 3. Pietro da Cortona, S. Maria della Pace (detail). Photo by Roger Scruton.

is the Order contained in the pattern books, and preserved in cornices, window surrounds, stringcourses, and door frames, in chimneys and railings, in all our city streets before the twentieth century. Even the most elaborate corner can be seen, therefore, to be the logical outcome of intelligible rules, so as to look less like an intrusion than a culmination. The example that I give, from Pietro da Cortona at S. Maria della Pace, shows exactly what I mean by the generative grammar of temple architecture (fig. 3). This exterior corner is seen as a form *arrived at*, not a form imposed, and arrived at through the generative power of the Order concealed within it. This is stone, but stone with a soul.

Traditional buildings have an orientation: they face the world, not always in one direction only, but in such a way as to address the space before them. They are not edges to the public space but visitors that congregate along it. Moreover, behind the facade, half-revealed through windows and suggested by doors and stringcourses, there is life. It is stretching things a bit to talk in this case of "visitation and transcendence," as Levinas does of the human face. But you can easily see why someone might be tempted to use this idiom. Our ability to endow buildings with faces is like our ability to see character in a theatrical mask. Buildings that face us acquire a face, an expression, of their own. And surely one of the most disturbing features of the modernist townscape is that all the buildings are faceless.

Needless to say, modern writers on architecture do not adopt Archeanassa's myth of origins. They do not see architecture as a consecration of the land in the name of the gods that are to dwell in it. All this, for the modern writer, is metaphor, and a metaphor that we should now abandon. Nevertheless, even in the twentieth century, serious efforts to capture the true significance of architecture have tended to discount function and utility, in favor of values that are deeply rooted in the psyche. For the followers of Melanie Klein, for example, architecture is a representation of the human body, and in particular of the body of the mother, loved and hated, needed and escaped from, bearing the inscription of our deepest anxieties and joys.[7] For Ruskin, architecture must be guided by the lamp of truth and the lamp of sacrifice, which point always to the idealized life of the spirit. Whenever philosophers and critics have thought seriously about the distinction between permanent architecture and a temporary shed, they have moved in Archeanassa's direction, identifying some deep and spiritual stratum of the human psyche as the source of the comfort we feel when things go right, and of our discomfort when things go wrong.

Archeanassa's myth should be rewritten, not as a story about the origins of architecture, but as a story about its essence. Towns are

---

[7] See, for example, Adrian Stokes, *Stones of Rimini* (London: Faber and Faber, 1934), and the discussion of Stokes and Klein in my *Aesthetics of Architecture* (Princeton, NJ: Princeton University Press, 1979), chap. 10.

homes to us when the buildings meet us face-to-face. Vernacular architecture from all periods and places has adapted to the human need for home and settlement, and in each case evolved some local variant of the standing posture, the smiling surface, and the fractal order common to growing things.[8] In the classical tradition these aesthetic constants are digested into grammar, to become generative principles of indefinitely many pleasing shapes and forms. The implied Order retains the calm and unobtrusive background of shapes that were (according to the myth) lifted out of nature and consecrated to the spirit. It is the visible license to dwell, the affirmation of our right of occupation, and the reminder that our communities precede and survive us.[9]

Before a sacred place or artifact I stand back in a posture of respect. This bit of the world, I believe, is inviolable. Just as the subject appears in the human face, and lays before the assassin and the abuser the absolute "no," so does an observing, questing, interrogating "I" appear in the sacred place, and command us to respect it. The experience of the sacred is interpersonal. Only creatures with "I" thoughts can see the world in this way, and their doing so depends upon a kind of interpersonal readiness, a willingness to find meanings and reasons, even in things that have no eyes to look at them and no mouth to speak. That, in my view, is what Alberti meant by the striving for *concinnitas*. True architects do not subdue their material to some external purpose; they *converse* with it, allowing the material to interrogate the space in which they build. Because we are subjects, the world looks back at us with a questioning regard, and we respond by organizing and conceptualizing it in other ways than those endorsed by science. The world as we live it is not the world as science explains it, any more than the smile of the *Mona Lisa* is a smear of pigments on a canvas. But this lived world is as real as the *Mona Lisa's* smile. And the same overreaching intentionality that informs our responses to the human face informs our responses to the human habitat, which comes to us as a place haunted by those who have made their home in it.

---

[8] See Nikos A. Salingaros, *A Theory of Architecture* (Solingen: Umbau-Verlag, 2006).
[9] Martin Heidegger, "Building, Dwelling, Thinking," in *Poetry, Language, Thought*, trans. Albert Hofstadter (New York: Harper Colophon, 1971).

A public space is not an unowned space, but one in which the many spheres of ownership come to a negotiated boundary. This boundary may be a street, a sequence of facades, or a skyline. It represents the side-by-side settlement of private owners, and the way of life that they share. Hence when the boundary is punctured or stolen by some private interest, we react to this as a desecration. This is especially true in cities, whose contours record a continuous dialogue over centuries between "neighbors"—those who "build nearby," to give the Anglo-Saxon etymology of the word. The culture of consumption sweeps across them like a tornado, scattering in its wake the doll-like images of advertising models, which wash up across the buildings and hide their face from view, as in the billboard- and digital-image-covered buildings of today's Bucharest, a city once described as "the Paris of the East."

The junk streets of modern cities should be contrasted with the jumbled compositions that arise by an invisible hand when traditional vernacular facades are forced to align themselves. Consider the backwater canals of Venice (fig. 4). These are transparently lived in,

Fig. 4. Venice canal. © FreeFoto.com.

and every detail has a use: but no detail was *dictated* by its use, and a pleasing redundancy inhabits each facade. Such examples help us to understand what was lost when the modernist vernacular took over, and the city of slabs replaced the city of columns. The "machine for living in" is not a subject but an object—a place in a fallen world.

Beauty and Settlement

We find ourselves here in philosophical territory that was mapped out by Kant in the *Critique of Judgement*. The topic of the first part of that book is the judgment of beauty—a judgment that we all make, and which we need to make, Kant believed, if we are to achieve a full understanding of the world and of our own rational capacities. Beauty resides in appearances, but appearances are also realities, and things that we share. Our interest in appearances stems from the desire to be at home in our surroundings, and to find inscribed in the world of objects some record of our personal concerns. It is in the world of appearances that we become what we truly are, and one proof of this is the human face—the place in which the human subject comes into view, and readies itself for others.

The *Critique of Pure Reason* established that appearances are not the passively received "impressions" of the empiricist myth, but the products of a profound interaction between subject and object, by which we impose form and order on the input received through our senses. In our everyday interaction with the world, the objects of experience come before us as "to be known" or "to be used." But there is another posture open to us, in which appearances are ordered as objects to be contemplated. In the experience of the beautiful we take the world into consciousness and let it float there. To put it another way: we savor the world, as something *given*, and not just as something received. This is not like the savoring of a taste or a smell: it involves a reflective study of meanings, and an attempt to find the human significance of the things that appear before us, *as* they appear. This savoring of impressions leads of its own accord to a critical attitude, and to reason-governed choices. I measure the object observed against the subject observing it and put both in question. In this way aesthetic interest is the culminating openness to the *Lebenswelt*: the way in which we look on the world as the *meaning of itself*.

Aesthetic values are intrinsic values, and when I find beauty in some object, it is because I am seeing it as an end in itself and not only as a means. And its intrinsic meaning for me lies in its way of coming before my perception, so as to challenge me in the here and now. That way of encountering objects in the world is importantly like my way of seeing persons, when they stand before me face-to-face and I recognize that I am accountable to them and they to me. In the aesthetic experience we have something like a face-to-face encounter with the world itself, and with the things that it contains, just as we have in the experience of sacred things and sacred places.[10]

Although, by definition, intrinsic values cannot be translated into utilitarian values, this does not mean that they have no utility. Consider friendship. Your friend is valuable to you as the thing that he is. To treat him as a means—to use him for your purposes—is to undo the friendship. And yet friends are useful: they provide help in times of need, and they amplify the joys of daily living. Friendship is supremely useful, so long as we do not think of it as useful. Likewise with the human habitat. We gain the benefits of building when we cease to aim for them, and study instead to fit part to part in proper harmony. *Concinnitas* is the mother of utility.

The subject of aesthetics took off when Kant and Hume simultaneously recognized (though on very different grounds) that aesthetic enjoyment involves a judgment. My pleasure is founded in a sense of the rightness of the object that I enjoy, as it is presented to my attention. Kant and Hume wrote in this connection of the "judgment of taste." That eighteenth-century way of expressing the point is misleading, since the word "taste" is now used to describe the most arbitrary of our preferences in food and drink. The point is better expressed in terms of the normative character of aesthetic choices. Our ordinary aesthetic judgments concern what is right and wrong, what fits and harmonizes, what looks and sounds appropriate. Dressing for a party, setting a table, decorating a room, and so on, are all aimed

---

[10] For further expansion of this theme, see Roger Scruton, *Beauty: A Very Short Introduction* (Oxford: Oxford University Press, 2009).

at the *right* appearance, and the pleasure taken is inseparable from the judgment that the thing looks as it should. There is an *internal* relation here, between preference and judgment. Hence, whether we like it or not (and most people nowadays don't like it), we become answerable to other rational beings for our aesthetic choices. Through these choices we are creating presences in the world of others; and what they think of the result is part of how it matters both to them and to us. This is not to say that we can *find* reasons for our choices, still less that we can find *justifying* reasons. But we are in some sense committed to the existence of those reasons, and the art of criticism consists in discovering paths to them.

Neither Kant nor Hume came up with an argument that could really underpin this search for "the standard of taste," though both had interesting and far-reaching things to say about it. But the phenomenon appears less mysterious, I believe, if we see it as arising from the I-You relationship, and from our intrinsic tendency toward accountability. Aesthetic judgment is a fundamental element in the posture described by the German romantics as *Heimkehr*—the turning for home. In designing our surroundings, we are bringing them within the sphere of accountability to others and theirs to us. And in that sense we are providing the world with a face. We deface the world when we scribble "me" all over it, and invite others to do the same. Beauty is the face of the community, and ugliness the attack on that face by the solipsist and the scavenger.

We shape our surroundings as a home by farming, by building, by arranging the world. Aesthetic values govern every form of settlement, and it is the nomads, those "passing through," who acknowledge no responsibility for the way things appear around them. The face of nature, as we see it in the great landscape paintings of Constable and Crome, of Courbet and Corot, is a face *turned toward us,* giving and receiving both frowns and smiles. And later artists showed another kind of expression, called forth onto the face of nature by the urgent desire to find what is *really there*, regardless of all the myths and stories. In the paintings of Van Gogh trees, flowers, orchards, fields, and buildings break open to the artist's brush, in something like the way that a human face can break open in response to a smile, to reveal an intense inner life and an affirmation of being. Throughout the nineteenth century artists, poets, and composers were in this way exploring and imploring the face of nature, eager for a direct and I-to-I encounter. The desire to perpetuate this face and to save it from unnecessary blemishes motivated the environmental movement, which was (in its origins, at least) the political expression of a profoundly romantic sensibility.[11]

If my argument in this chapter is right, it can be generalized to cover the entire human habitat: not the city only, but the environment in which it is placed, and the landscape round about. Environmental degradation comes in just the same way that moral degradation comes, through representing people and places in impersonal ways, as objects to be used rather than as subjects to be respected. The sense of beauty puts a brake upon destruction, by representing its object as irreplaceable. When the world looks back at me with my eyes, as it does in aesthetic experience, it is also addressing me in another way. Something is being revealed to me, and I am being made to stand still and absorb it. It is of course nonsense to suggest that there are naiads in the trees and dryads in the groves. What is revealed to me in the experience of beauty is a fundamental truth about being—that being is a gift.

[11] See Roger Scruton, *Green Philosophy: How to Think Seriously about the Planet* (London: Atlantic, 2012).

7

The Sacred Space of Music

The argument of the two previous chapters contains a suggestion about the sacred, namely, that it comes to us as part of the "overreaching intentionality" of our interpersonal states of mind. The embodied form of the other, as this comes before us in love, anger, and desire, is understood as a revelation. The other haunts his body, and is revealed in it, not as something seen in a window, but as something that flits out of sight, inhabiting the "space of reasons" alone.[1] The many French philosophers who have meditated on the role of the "other" in our attitudes and states of mind have, I think, had this experience in mind.[2] They have recognized that, while there is an ordinary sense in which everything in my world that is not me is other than me, there is also a class of entities in my world that are *actively* other: whose otherness consists in the fact that I in my turn am other to them. In the gaze of such another I am isolated, summoned into myself, and held to account. And I look on the other in just the same way. It is this "overreaching intentionality" that we carry with us in our search for home, and which ensures, in Saint Augustine's famous words, that our hearts are restless, until they rest in Thee.

I explored the way in which this overreaching intentionality goes in search of meaning, not only in the face and form of the human being, but in the world of everyday objects, and the places of pilgrimage where we wish to be at home. And I connected that phenomenon with the cognitive dualism that I have been defending in the course of this book. Our twofold way of viewing the human being extends

[1] I borrow the expression "the space of reasons" from Sellars: see the argument of chap. 2.

[2] The cult of the Other in French postwar philosophy should be traced to Hegel, through Kojève's lectures, delivered 1934 onward, collected by Raymond Queneau, *Introduction à la lecture de Hegel* (Paris: Gallimard, 1946). But see especially "The Existence of Others," in Sartre's *Being and Nothingness*, trans. Hazel E. Barnes (London: Routledge, 1953), pp 235–45.

outward into the world of objects, and lays claim to it as ours: *Welt* and *Lebenswelt* contain the same material, organized in two contrasting forms. For we are home-building creatures—*Der Mensch ist ein heimatliches Wesen*, as the philosopher Karen Joisten has put it[3]—and we seek to impress ourselves on our surroundings and to receive endorsement and security from the place where we are. That, I maintain, is the origin of the aesthetics of everyday life, to which I devoted a few remarks at the end of the previous chapter.

The aesthetic impulse is a high point in our demand that the world be meaningful to us, so as to correspond, in some deep way, to the interpersonal intentionality with which we address our surroundings. The study of this aspect of the human condition was a fundamental part, perhaps the most fundamental part, of the humanities, in the period when these emerged from philology as topics of university study. And it is worth returning again to the current attempts to downgrade or dismiss humane understanding, or to replace it with a natural science of the human being, so as to situate man in the order of nature, and not in the interpersonal world. For what I go on to say will depend firmly on old forms of thought, and old methods of argument, that have been developed, and in my view successfully developed, in the various disciplines of humane scholarship during the last two centuries.

Scientism and Human Understanding

Until recently it has been assumed that, if there is a method in the humanities, it is not the method of science. We don't understand the plays of Shakespeare by conducting surveys and experiments. We don't interpret *The Art of Fugue* with an acoustical analysis, or Michelangelo's *David* with the crystallography of marble. Art, literature, music, and history belong to the *Lebenswelt*, the world that is shaped by our own consciousness, and we study them not by explaining how they arose but by interpreting what they mean. Explanation has a method, and it is the method of science. Interpretation goes in *search* of a method, but

[3] *Philosophie der Heimat: Heimat der Philosophie* (Berlin: Akademie Verlag, 2003).

is never sure of finding one. Since the early nineteenth century strong claims have been made on behalf of "hermeneutics," "phenomenology," "structuralism"—disciplines that promise the missing "method" through which meaning is discovered and explored. But the claims have a tendency to evaporate on examination, so as to become special pleading on behalf of a particular set of authorities, a particular cultural inheritance, or a particular aesthetic taste.

Over the last two decades, however, Darwinism has invaded the field of the humanities, in a way that Darwin himself would scarcely have predicted. Doubt and hesitation have given way to certainty, interpretation has been subsumed into explanation, and the whole realm of aesthetic experience and literary judgment has been brought to heel as an "adaptation," a part of human biology which exists because of the benefit that it confers on our genes. No need now to puzzle over the meaning of music or the nature of beauty in art. The meaning of art and music reside in what they do for our genes. Once we see that these features of the human condition are adaptations, acquired perhaps many thousands of years ago, during the time of our hunter-gatherer ancestors, we will be able to explain them. We will know what art and music essentially *are* by discovering what they do.

Take music, for example. A mother singing to her child creates a bond through her singing. The two rock back and forth to its rhythm; the sound is internalized by the child as mother's sound, the sound of safety. A woman who can bond with her child in that way gives the child an added source of security, and the two cling to each other more firmly when the moment of crisis arrives. So the singing mother confers, through her singing, a tiny reproductive advantage on the genes that produced her music—just enough to ensure that, over a few hundred generations, the singing humans prevail over their tone-deaf competitors.

Or take the sense of beauty. Why does it exist, and what does it do for us? The problem is likened to that of the peacock's tail (for example, by Geoffrey Miller).[4] Why does this bird squander its resources,

---

[4]Geoffrey Miller, *The Mating Mind* (New York: Random House, 2000). The problem of the peacock's tail is usefully connected with that of the self-sacrificing ant by Helena Cronin, in *The Ant and the Peacock: Altruism and Sexual Selection from Darwin to Today* (Cambridge: Cambridge University Press, 1991).

encumber its flight, and generally make a gift of itself to predators, just to show off a vast array of pretty feathers? The answer is that prettiness counts. It counts as a sign of reproductive fitness: superfluous attributes are carried by extra-energetic organisms. Hence if peahens distinguish peacocks through the size of their tails, they will also, unknowingly but reliably, be discriminating on grounds of reproductive fitness. Their genes will be more likely to be passed on if they go for the cock with the tail, and evolutionary pressure will therefore make the tails get bigger and bigger until the wretched birds topple over from the weight of them. And just in that way, we are told, men tattoo themselves, make pictures, write poems, so advertising through these functionless pursuits the squandered biological resources that permit them. Women fall for artists for the same reason that peahens fall for glamorous tails.

Gradually the humanities are being invaded and disciplined by explanations of that kind, which purport to sweep away the mess of hermeneutics and replace it with clean, meaningful science. And the explanations really are as absurd as the two examples I have given— absurd precisely because they are looking to explain something that they have not defined. Until you define what music *is*, and how it differs from pitched sound, for example, you will not know what question you are asking, when you inquire into its origins. Until you recognize that the human sense of beauty is a completely different thing from the peahen's sexual attraction, you won't know what, if anything, is proved by the sparse similarities. You will describe present human motivation as though it were "nothing but" its hypothetical archetype, and instead of a science of human development you will produce a new myth of origins, and one from which everything distinctively human has been cast aside.

Worse, the whole "adaptation" approach to human phenomena is topsy-turvy. It involves an application, case by case, of the theory of natural selection, as supplemented by modern genetics. It tells us that, if a trait is widespread across our species, then it has been "selected for." But this means only that the trait is *not maladaptive*, that it is not something that would disappear under evolutionary pressure. And that is a trivial observation. Of everything that exists it could be said that it has not disappeared under evolutionary pressure. That tells us nothing about how the thing in question came to exist. Nor does it tell us anything about its meaning or significance for us. The attempt to explain art, music, literature, and the sense of beauty as adaptations is surely both trivial as science and empty as a form of understanding. It tells us nothing of importance about its subject matter, and does huge intellectual damage in persuading people that after all there is nothing about the humanities to *understand*, since they have all been *explained*—and explained away. (Which is, incidentally, the line taken by Alex Rosenberg in *The Atheist's Guide to Reality*, 2011.)

Understanding Music

One of the most important facts about music, therefore, is that it is a thing to be *understood*, and understanding music is not a matter of exploring neural pathways or acoustical relations, but a matter of attending to and grasping the intrinsic order and meaning of events in musical space. Furthermore music is an *appearance*. If you look for music in the order of nature, you will not find it. Of course, you will find sounds, which is to say pitched vibrations, caused as a rule by human activity, and impinging on the ears of those who listen to them. But you won't find any of the features that distinguish *music*. For example, you won't find the space in which music moves. You won't find the gravitational forces that bring melodies to rest or make the notes of a chord cohere as a single entity. You won't find melodies—those strange things that begin and end and move through musical space between their vivid edges. You won't find tones—the elements from which melodies are composed—but only the pitched sounds in which we hear them. Music is all appearance, and yet it is not an illusion or a passing veneer that we could fail to notice and be none the worse for not noticing. It is *out there* and not *in here*, to use the familiar metaphors—though note that they are metaphors, which might be both illuminating and misleading when it comes to spelling them out. This is part of what I tried to show in chapter 2, and it is worth returning briefly to the example that I used in that chapter (ex. 1).

The sequence of sounds that you hear at the start of Beethoven's Third Piano Concerto are not heard simply as a sequence. They contain a movement, and this movement is in musical space. It is not movement of the kind you observe in machines or even in animals. It is an expression of intention—the intention contained in the music (which is not necessarily a private intention of the composer's). Put it another way: this is a movement of which you can, at any point, ask "why?" Why, for example does it descend stepwise from the G, having got there by a leaping arpeggio? Why, having got back to the starting point, does it proceed to emphasize its being there with two dominant to tonic punctuation marks? You might find these questions difficult to answer. But they make sense, just as though they were asked of human actions. The two commas are there to complete the phrase, to establish closure in the mind of the listener, to prepare the way for another and answering movement that will move everything forward into another key. And why do that? That question too has an answer. The whole theme unfolds through questions and answers, like a game of chess, and this gives substance to the widespread feeling that a work like this is saying something—though not something that could be put into words.

Many people dismiss the idea of musical movement, or at least try to replace it with something that seems more in keeping with the reality—for example, the loss of tension that accompanies the return to the tonic, or the harmonic expectations that accumulate through a musical line. But these descriptions are no less metaphorical than the idea of musical movement, and besides are applicable only to a certain kind of music. There is movement through musical space in atonal music, and there are melodies—pentatonic melodies, for example—that maintain a uniform harmonic tension throughout, yet which nevertheless move.

Musical movement is, or seems to be, goal directed. That is to say, it moves toward definite closures or half-closures, and these again cannot be easily explained in terms of harmonic tension. They are events "in the space of reasons." The classical idiom uses this fact to generate an idea of musical progress and accomplishment: a movement grows out of the thematic material, and moves through musical space in search of its completion. And this presents us with something that we do not encounter in everyday life, which is too much troubled by randomness—namely, the completed gesture, the gesture that completes *itself* out of its own inner content, which has no purpose but itself and yet which also *accomplishes* that purpose. For many people this is the central mystery, and the most important reward, of serious music—that it shows us human action drawing itself to a close.

Musical movement also has a kind of internal necessity—or at least, it tends in this direction. In *The Art of Fugue* Bach explores the many ways in which musical gestures generate their own aura of necessity, so that what follows seems compelled, and seems also in turn to compel its successor. This is so, even though at every point there may be indefinitely many syntactically possible ways of going on. Necessity, here, is as though won out of freedom, rather than the other way round. Again we find it difficult to describe this process without the use of extended metaphors—question and answer, premise and inference, for example. But this sense of compulsion is so important to our experience of music that we are apt to criticize a piece when it is absent, and find ourselves irritated by redundancies and arbitrary digressions that seem to have nothing to do with the musical argument.

The Space of Music

This sense of compulsion should be understood in connection with the intentionality of musical movement. In music we find actions that are both necessary and free. Music is a perceived resolution of the conflict between freedom and necessity, made available in a space of its own. Presented with that description of music, you might well ask whether it is a description of something real. To which I answer yes, though it is a reality that cannot be grasped from the ordinary cognitive standpoint. No science, no theory, no form of explanation with which we order and predict the physical world, could possibly make contact with the movement that we hear when we hear a melody in musical space, and geometrical mappings of musical relations are not, in my view, accounts of musical space.[5]

[5]*Pace* Tymoczko, *A Geometry of Music*. See again my review of Tymoczko, *Reason Papers* (2012).

You can see this very plainly if you ask yourself just what it is that moves, when music moves. The melody of the Beethoven began on C and moved up to E-flat. But what moved? Not C, which is stuck forever at C. Nor did anything release itself from that C and travel to E-flat—there is no musical ectoplasm that travels across the void between the semitones. If you go on pushing questions like those, you will soon come to the conclusion that there is something contradictory in the idea that a note can move along the pitch spectrum—no note can be identified independently of the place that it occupies, which makes it seem as though the idea of a *place* is in some way illegitimate. In all kinds of ways musical space defies our ordinary understanding of movement: for example, octave equivalence means that a theme can return to its starting point even though moving constantly upward—a kind of Escher paradox, which has no equivalent in ordinary geometry. Musical space has other interesting topological features. For example, things can rarely be moved through musical space in such a way as to coincide with their mirror image, any more than the left hand, to take Kant's famous example, can be turned in physical space so as to coincide with the right hand. Thus no asymmetrical chord can be transposed onto its mirror form.

The net result of those and similar reflections is to conclude that nothing *literally* moves in musical space, but that in some way the idea of space cannot be eliminated from our experience of music. We are dealing with an entrenched metaphor—but not a metaphor of words, exactly, for we are not talking about how people describe music; we are talking about how they *experience* it. It is as though there is a metaphor of space and movement *embedded within* our experience and cognition of music. This metaphor cannot be "translated away," and what it says cannot be said in the language of physics—for example, by talking instead of the pitches and timbre of sounds in physical space. Yet what it describes, the musical movement, is a real presence—and not just for me: for anyone with a musical ear.

There is nothing mysterious here, once we admit the kind of cognitive dualism that I have been defending. Nor should it surprise us that the terms that we apply to music place it firmly in the arena of personal life. It moves as *we* move, with reasons for what it does and a sense of purpose (which might at any moment evaporate, like the purposes of people). It has the outward appearance of the inner life, so to speak, and although it is heard and not seen, it is heard as the voice is heard, and understood like the face—as a revelation of free subjectivity. Unlike us, however, music creates the space in which it moves. And that space is ordered by fields of force that seem to be radiated from the notes that occur in them.

Consider the chord: perhaps the most mysterious of all musical entities. Not every collection of notes makes a chord—not even if they are notes from the same consonant triad. (Thus in the "Hostias" of Berlioz's *Grande messe des morts*, in which a B-flat minor triad on flutes is separated by four octaves from the B-flat on trombones, that last-mentioned B-flat seems not to belong to the chord at all, despite being its fundamental.) In much modern music we do not hear chords but only "simultaneities," sounds of distinct pitch and timbre that happen to coincide, but between which there is an empty space—often a haunted space, as in the atonal works of Schoenberg. A chord, whether consonant or dissonant, fills the musical space between its edges. And it faces other musical objects from those edges. You can stuff more notes into it, but in doing so you are making it more dense, not occupying space that is not already occupied. And here is another peculiarity of musical space: that two objects can be in the same space at the same time, as when contrapuntal voices briefly coincide on a single pitch, or when two chords are superimposed and each retains its separate gestalt, as in polytonal music. Chords have distinctive relations to the fields of force in which they are suspended. They can be soft and sloppy, like thirteenth chords in jazz—and that regardless of their dissonance. They can be hard and tight, like the final chords of a Beethoven symphony—and that regardless of their consonance. They can yield to their neighbors, lead into them or away from them, or they might stand out as sharp and unrelated.

Musical Culture

It is clear, or ought to be clear, that music does not work as language works: it is not organized by semantic rules that enable us to assign an interpretation to every musical utterance in the way that we assign a meaning to every utterance in a language. And this point was importantly emphasized by Eduard Hanslick in his book *The Beautiful in Music*, designed as a rebuke to the extravagant claims of the Wagnerians, on behalf of music's expressive power.

Now any approach to the question of musical meaning today will immediately come up against a skeptical question: what kind of music are you talking about? And why aren't you talking about *my* kind of music? A species of vigilant censorship is maintained on behalf of popular taste, and to break through it you have to establish your political entitlement in some other way.[6] The most famous triumph in this respect is that of the Frankfurt School critic Theodor Adorno who, coming as a refugee to Hollywood in the 1930s, repaid the vast hospitality of which he was a recipient by pouring scorn on the people who offered it, and in particular on the entertainment industry to which he imagined them to be enslaved.[7]

Adorno's attack on jazz and the jazz-based idiom of the American songbook did not concern itself directly with the music—about which he had hardly a word to say. It concerned itself with listening, and what listening meant, now that mass communication could attract ears in every household. He believed that listening had changed, so as to demand the short-range melodies and cluttered harmonic progressions that he attributed (without examination, it must be said) to songs in the jazz idiom. There had been, as he put it, a "regression" of listening, a retreat from the great adventures placed before it by the classical symphonic tradition, into the short-breathed exhalations that demand little or nothing by way of a response.

We must surely recognize that there is a great difference between a musical culture based in serious listening to extended movements of highly intricate musical thought, and a musical culture based in hearing largely predictable melodies, supported by mechanical rhythms and off-the-shelf harmonies, which quickly exhaust their sparse musical potential. The rise of the new mass culture has not happened in

---

[6]This is not the place to confront the advocates of musical ecumenism—anybody interested in what I have to say about pop can consult the article "Soul Music," which appeared online in the *American* for 27 February 2010, http://www.american.com/archive/2010/february/soul-music, and which comes complete with musical examples and music videos.

[7]See my "Why Read Adorno?" in *Understanding Music* (London: Continuum, 2009).

the realm of music only. Vast social and political changes can be read into this transition, and Adorno was surely right to notice this. We may not agree with Adorno's critical judgment. After all, he was dismissing *everything*: not jazz only, but the American musical and songbook that were born out of jazz; the synthesis of jazz and concert-hall music that you find in Gershwin's *Rhapsody in Blue*, in Stravinsky's Concerto for Piano and Wind Instruments, in Ravel's G major Piano Concerto, and in a hundred other beautiful and exuberant works in "serious" mode; indelible melodies like Jerome Kern's "All the Things You Are," Richard Rodgers's "Some Enchanted Evening," Cole Porter's "Night and Day," and so on. But it is surely plausible to argue, as Adorno did, that the ways of listening were altered by the rise of the mass media. The process that began in his day has continued, to the extent that it is often unclear today whether music is to be listened to or merely overheard, or maybe even just *looked at*, as the sound effects fill the background of a gripping video.

Nobody can doubt the importance of music in our civilization, both as a source of communal bonding and as an object of solitary consolation. People are shaped by the things they listen to and the recreations they enjoy, and Plato was surely right to regard the Corybants of his time with a measure of suspicion. Adorno shared Plato's qualms for other reasons—notably because he saw the new American music as the enemy of autonomous thought, a kind of captivating addiction that resulted in the enslavement of its devotees. And although Adorno was surely wrong about Cole Porter, Jerome Kern, Richard Rodgers, George Gershwin, Hoagy Carmichael, and all the others whose songs still find an echo in ordinary human hearts, he was making an important point that is relevant to what I have been arguing in this chapter.

Mass Culture and Addiction

To understand the point, it is useful to return to a matter that I discussed in chapter 5—the intentionality of sexual desire. The civilizations that we know have incorporated sex into extended, sometimes lifelong projects of union between people. Sex has been absorbed, as

I argued, into the world of vows, rather than that of contracts, and contractual sex, like recreational sex, has been accepted only with a form of ritual condemnation. In the world in which we live, a new kind of sexual norm has emerged, in which the overreaching intentionality of the interpersonal relation is curtailed. The sexual object replaces the sexual subject, and often, as in pornography, this object is reduced to a mere body part, or—to use the vulgar expression—a tool. This instrumentalizing approach cancels the other's reality as a subject, and, when used to arouse and satisfy some kind of sexual urge, it removes sexual pleasure entirely from the I-You relation, there being, in this case, neither an I nor a You. What is interesting, from the psychological point of view, is that the resulting experience is addictive—that is to say, it can be obtained without effort, leads automatically to the pleasure that completes it, and rapidly colonizes the brain of the one who gives way to it. (See the recently established *Journal of Sex Addiction* for the psychological consequences.)

Something similar has happened with music, in which the "quick fix" has driven out the sympathetic response, and in which the I-You intentionality is no longer the focus of attention. In disco music, for example, the focus is entirely on repeated rhythmical figures, often synthesized digitally and without any clear musical performance, in which musical arousal is brought to an instant narcissistic climax and thereafter repeated. There is neither melody nor harmonic progression, but merely repetition, demanding no effort of listening and divorced from any relation with the external world. Those who dance to this music do not, as a rule dance *with* their partners, supposing they have partners, but *at* them, for the simple reason that there is no "with" established by the musical line. The music is machinelike, not in its sound only, but in its mode of production and in its bypassing of all interpersonal relations, to focus on the pure stimulus and the pure response. It is a music of objects, from which subjects have been excluded. (If you want an example, try Technohead, "I Wanna Be a Hippy," and don't miss out on the video.)

That is one of those aspects of music that we don't find surprising until we think about them. From the dance of the Israelites around the golden calf to the orgies of hip-hop, the musical distractions of ordinary people have called down the maledictions of their priestly guardians. The priests have throughout history tried not merely to control what is sung and played in the temple, but to confine and if necessary forbid the revels that take place outside. We no longer think we can do this by law, as Plato wished. But we are still deeply concerned by changes in musical practice, in just the way that Moses was, when he descended from the mountain and, on seeing the idolatry of the masses, cast the tablets of the law to the ground.

That was perhaps the first recorded protest against "mass culture." Adorno is a latter-day Moses, and his hero Arnold Schoenberg tried to set the episode from the Old Testament to music, as an illustration of the way in which we must never sacrifice difficult truth to easy communication. In the contrast between Moses and Aaron in Schoenberg's unfinished (and surely unfinishable) opera, we see dramatized the clash of cultures that preoccupied Adorno. There is a culture of long-term thought and abstract conception, represented by Moses; and a culture of short-term pleasure and easy communication, represented by Aaron. The first points us to the transcendental ground of being; the second reduces beings to idols. Schoenberg's treatment of this theme reminds us that many of the worries concerning the depravities of popular musical culture reflect the fear of idolatry—of false gods, false worship, and false emotions.

Adorno wanted to show that the freedoms seemingly enjoyed by the American people are illusory freedoms, and that the underlying cultural reality is one of enslavement—enslavement to the fetishes of the market and the consumer culture, which by placing appetite above long-term values lead to the loss of rational autonomy. Popular music was not, for Adorno, something that Americans had been liberated *to*, but something that they must be liberated *from*. In short, he was, in his own eyes, an iconoclast, freeing the people from the dominion of their idols.

The Meaning of Silence

We are clearly in deep water here; and we are not going to save ourselves simply by taking the kind of nonjudgmental approach that is so often promoted by courses in music appreciation. In this area to be nonjudgmental is already to make a kind of judgment: it is to suggest that it really doesn't matter what you listen to or dance to, and that there are no moral distinctions among the various listening habits that have emerged in the age of mechanical reproduction. That is a morally charged position, and one that flies in the face of common sense. To suggest that people who live with a mechanical rhythmic pulse as a constant background to their thoughts and movements are living *in the same way*, with the same kind of attention and the same pattern of challenges and rewards, as others who know music only from sitting down to listen to it, clearing their minds, meanwhile, of all other thoughts—such a suggestion is wildly implausible.

Put laconically, the difference between those two ways of responding to music is the difference between preventing silence, and letting silence speak. Music in the listening culture is a voice that arises out of silence, and which uses silence as a painter uses the canvas: silence is the *prima materia* from which the work is composed, and the most eloquent parts of the classical sonata movement are often the parts when nothing can be heard, when, for however brief a moment, we hear *through* the music to the silence behind, as in the recitatives of Beethoven's D minor Sonata, op. 31, no. 2, known sometimes as "The Tempest." Themes can be punctuated by silences in which the expressive burden is somehow greater than that borne by the notes. A very good example of this is the theme used by Elgar for the *Enigma Variations*, in which the sighing strings are constantly held up as though by a hand from the silence, and then finally pushed aside by the counter-theme in the major key, stepping from behind, as it were, and filling all the available space.

There are those who say that the listening culture is time-bound and inessential, that it is merely one *use* to which music can be put, and that in other times and other places music has meaning in other ways. I don't doubt that there is a truth in this. However, there are two important qualifications to be made. First, we should recognize that music is not something independent of the way in which we respond to it. I argued that what we hear in the opening theme of Beethoven's Third Piano Concerto is not just a sequence of pitched sounds, but a movement in musical space, responding to gravitational forces that control and propel it. Someone might not hear this movement; and it is plausible to say that it is properly understood only by the person who listens in the right way, obedient to the constraints that transform sound into tone. In this sense, listening is not a practice that could be subtracted from our music, while leaving the music unchanged. It is as necessary to the nature of music as the I-You relation is necessary to our nature as persons. Music, like people, is a relational fact.

Second, although it is true that music has many uses, these uses are forms of listening. You will hear people say that the concert-hall culture of the Western metropolis is nevertheless something rarefied and abstracted, and that the natural form taken by music is as an accompaniment to human activity, whether in dancing, marching, working, or preparing for war. And, as I indicated earlier, the evolutionary psychologists will be first to step in here, assimilating music to one or other of the wider strategies that further the reproduction of our genes. However, these "other uses" of music are extensions of the art of listening. And it has been true since ancient times and in all cultures that the peculiar power of music is most noticeable *not* when we are dancing to it or singing along, but precisely when the pure tone arrests us and we stand to listen. Thus it is instrumental music that forms the core of the classical Indian raga and the Balinese gamelan, and also of the all-but-forgotten classical music of China and Japan. The ancient discussions concerning the power of music and the contest between the Apollonian and Dionysian forces that seek expression in it was mythologized in terms of the lyre and the aulos. It was the *lyre* of Orpheus, not his voice, that moved the beasts and the stones.

In the tenth sonnet of the second book of *Sonnets to Orpheus* Rilke, acknowledging the threat posed by the machine and by every kind of instrumental way of seeing things, summons the music of Orpheus as the proof that we still live in a consecrated world:

> Being is still enchanted for us; in a hundred
> Places it remains a source—a play of pure
> Powers, which no one touches, who does not kneel and wonder.

> Words still go softly forth towards the unsayable,
> And music, always new, from palpitating stones
> Builds in useless space its godly home.

The space of music is useless, since nothing solid stands in it. The house that music builds is made from palpitating stones (*bebendsten Steinen*)—life-stones, made of breath and thought. And just as words go out toward the thing they cannot touch or meet—toward the subject that no words can encompass—so does music go out into a space beyond the order of nature, where untouchable things reside. When we listen to pure instrumental music, we often have this impression: and it seems then that the music is telling us something of the first importance, revealing something about our world that perhaps cannot be stated or explained, but only intimated in the pure language of tones.

The Meaning of Music

Is there anything more precise that we can say about the meaning of music—more precise than the wonderful invocation contained in Rilke's metaphors? I think there is. But first we must recognize some of the difficulties. Those who have most eagerly defended the meaningfulness of music have described music as an expressive medium—implying that, in some way, our emotions inhabit the music, and that we, encountering them there, are moved to sympathy and understanding. I don't say that that is wrong, but it needs careful exposition if we are to understand exactly what it means.

The first problem, pointed out by Hanslick, is that there is a seeming contradiction between the thought that music expresses emotion and the claim that it is an abstract (or, as was then said, absolute) art form.[8] The romantics who defended absolute music as the liberation of music from the distracting uses of dance, opera, and song, extolled the pure "thought sound" of instrumental music, just as the followers of Orpheus might have done. For them the soul breathed in a Beethoven symphony or quartet with a pure sound of its own, divorced from the compromises of action. But, argued Hanslick, emotions, like other states of mind, are *about* things. And how can

[8] Eduard Hanslick, *The Beautiful in Music: A Contribution to the Revisal of Musical Aesthetics*, trans. Gustav Cohen (New York: Novello, Ewer and Co., 1891).

music capture this aboutness if it is a purely abstract art? Moreover, doesn't all suggestion that it *should* capture some kind of aboutness detract from the essence of music, which is an art of pure sound, or rather "forms moved in sounding," as Hanslick put it? People who want to attach pictures, stories, and characters to *The Art of Fugue*, for example, seem to us not to have understood its meaning—its monumental presence in the world of tones, standing above and beyond the human world on a serene throne of authority.

There are two responses to that which deserve refutation. The first is to say that music can, so to speak, borrow its aboutness. Even purely instrumental music can acquire a subject matter in this way, and nobody has the slightest difficulty in hearing titles like *Blown Away Leaves, Vltava, The Lark Ascending, La Mer* as appropriate to the pieces that they name. The second response is to argue that music can imitate our states of mind, bypassing their specific intentionality, and reproducing their dynamic properties, thereby eliciting in us a lively sense of being in the presence of emotions whose precise objects we do not need to define in order to feel their gravitational pull. Music shares the moral and emotional aspect of human beings, and its significance lies in this fact.

Those two responses purport to solve the mystery of musical meaning while in fact merely distracting us from it. In answer to the first of them, let us take an example—the great orchestral tone poem by Rachmaninov that bears the title *The Isle of the Dead*, taken from the well-known evocative painting (or rather series of paintings) by Arnold Böcklin (fig. 5). A naive account of this piece might tell us that it is a description in tones of the very thing that Böcklin depicts in oils. But that misses the whole point of the title. Böcklin's painting displays a sepulchral island, set in a still sea, illuminated by the light of a setting sun, and visited by a shrouded figure from whom all individuality has been erased. This figure stands erect in a boat rowed by another who clearly does not belong in this place of no return. The picture is not a depiction of death, but an expression of feelings about death that are known to all of us. A trifle melodramatic perhaps, but conveying a sense of bleak and irreversible calamity. That, we might think, is what death is like, insofar as it is like anything. This is death seen not as an event in the order of nature, but as the impassable edge

Fig. 5. Arnold Böcklin, *Isle of the Dead*, first version, 1880. Basel, Kunstmuseum.
© 2013. DeAgostini Picture Library/SCALA, Florence.

of the *Lebenswelt*—our final isolation in a place where only impotent memories can reach us from the world of the living.

Rachmaninov's piece is not an attempt to depict Böcklin's island: how could music do such a thing? The rocks, the gloomy cypresses, the mouths of tombs, the strange light of a sun sinking on some unseen horizon—how can these things find their embodiment in sound? The music can capture the movement of the boat, certainly, for movement is something that we hear in music. But it is precisely in this connection that Rachmaninov allows music to depart on a course of its own. He builds the entire first part of the piece out of a kind of asymmetrical rowing motion in 5/4 time—two beats followed by three, and sometimes reversing the cut so that three beats are followed by two. On this he erects a solemn motive on consecutive notes that gradually takes in the whole orchestra, swelling a single A minor triad into a kind of bloated corpse of itself (ex. 2). The

Ex. 2. Rachmaninov, *The Isle of the Dead*.

harmony changes to D minor, and a hollow call from the horn answers like a fading memory of life. Then a burst of high diminished chords on violins and woodwind take flight like startled birds from the rock-like harmonies on the brass. All this is wonderfully evocative. It points us to contexts in which these devices have been linked to precise thoughts and events, and later the quotation of the first four notes of the "Dies Irae" reinforces these links. But nothing is actually *described*, and someone could follow the musical argument and never experience the evocative power of the music in the way that I have indicated.

You might very well say that this piece expresses an emotion that is close to that expressed by Böcklin's picture—that they exhibit what we might call expressive similarity or even expressive identity. But suppose someone did not get it—suppose he denied that the music evoked for him anything similar to the feelings evoked by Böcklin's painting. Would it follow that he had misunderstood the music? You might want to say that he had missed something. But suppose he follows intently the musical movement, and the impressive way in which the sparse material is developed, to a climax that is purely musical and which has no equivalent in the painting. Is that not a sign of musical understanding? And conversely, suppose someone notices all the references to death, makes all the links with Böcklin's painting, but is unable to follow the musical argument, gets lost in the rhythm, doesn't feel the musical impulse as it builds to the climax—shouldn't we say that he had not understood the piece?

The point I am getting at is this. If the meaning of Rachmaninov's piece lies in part in the thoughts and feelings expressed toward the object brought to mind by Böcklin's painting, then understanding the piece should involve recuperating those thoughts and feelings. But it would seem that we could understand the piece as music without any such mental recuperation. Likewise we could have a good idea of the thoughts and feelings that Rachmaninov is seeking to evoke, without understanding the musical argument. We should do well here to recall the nineteenth-century habit, associated with A. B. Marx, of assigning narrative programs to the Beethoven symphonies and sonatas. Those narratives are now forgotten or revisited only with ridicule: we think of them as describing the private fantasies of their author, but not the public meaning of the work.

It is undeniable that we apply terms denoting emotion and character to music: I have just done so, in describing our experience of the Rachmaninov. There is sad, joyful, bitter, hesitant, noble, passionate, and diffident music. And many philosophers have used this fact to propose a generalized intentionality in the musical experience, arguing that music provides the equivalent in sound of the human passions, moving in the same way or with the same dynamic stresses as we ourselves move under the pressure of emotion. The problem, as I see it, is that all those descriptions are figurative. And they don't serve to distinguish music from the other things that we describe in figurative terms. We speak of the noble oak tree, the sad cypress, the dancing willow, the gloomy pine—but these descriptions merely brush the surface of the things they touch like leaves blown across a path.

Meaning and Metaphor

There is a familiar move in the philosophy of music that tries to ground metaphor in analogy. It goes something like this: we begin from the question what does it mean to describe a piece of music as sad, noble, and so on? We respond with a suggestion: we mean that the music is *like* a sad or noble person. In what way like? Here I refer you to some of Peter Kivy's writings on the subject, which tell us that sad music shares the dynamic properties of sad people, it is slow-moving, drooping, ponderous, and so on.[9] And noble music is upstanding, fully presented, with straightforward gestures and clear, honest cadences. Then I want to protest, wait a moment, you haven't advanced us one bit: you said that sad music shares properties with sad people; and then you proved this by describing those properties in two ways—using literal language of people, and figurative language of the music. Music doesn't *literally* move slowly, droop, or ponder. The analogy turns out not to be an analogy at all, but a way of replacing one metaphor with another. I still have the question, what do these metaphors *mean*, and what do they tell me about the thing to which they are applied? And there is a strong tradition of argument, beginning with Wittgenstein's *Philosophical Investigations*, which says that you don't explain the meaning of a metaphor by looking at the metaphorical use, but by looking at the literal use. The thing that needs explaining is not the *meaning* of the word "sad," "noble," or whatever, but the purpose of using just that word in just this context. And whatever the purpose, it is not that of describing or picking out analogies.

But suppose these analogies exist. Suppose you can give sense to an emotion term or virtue word when used of music, by pointing to similarities between the work of music and the mental state or disposition referred to by the literal usage. Would this show that the term identifies something aesthetically interesting and morally relevant in the thing to which it applies? My answer is no. Everything resembles everything else, and most resemblances are insignificant; what makes resemblance interesting is the context that puts it to a use. You may have a striking resemblance to Elvis Presley. But, because you can't sing, can't move in a sexy way, can't do anything to put your resemblance on display, it remains insignificant. We notice many resemblances in music. The opening theme of Beethoven's op.

[9] *The Corded Shell: Reflections on Musical Expression* (Princeton, NJ: Princeton University Press, 1981), for example.

18, no. 1 is like someone signing a check: boldly putting down the hand, and then lapsing into a squiggle. But that resemblance (supposing we allow it) has nothing to do with the music or what it means. Naturally, therefore, we need to distinguish accidental from significant resemblances: and that is precisely what we cannot do, if the only ground for the use of mental predicates to describe music is the kind of analogy pointed to by Kivy.

To put the point simply: hearing the sadness of the music is not hearing an analogy between the music and an emotion: it is hearing the sadness *in* the music. To hear sadness in the music is to hear the contours of sadness in the music, true. But the features that we hear *in* the music are not necessarily features that the music shares. Indeed, I contend that they are in this case features (drooping, heaviness, weariness) that it *cannot* literally share. So in explaining what it is to hear sadness in the music, we have simply helped ourselves to the very notion that needs to be explained—the notion of hearing x in y, when x is a feature that y cannot literally possess.

So what goes on when we hear sadness *in* the music? We are dealing with a metaphorical perception—hearing the music under a concept that does not literally apply to it.[10] And we do this by directing toward the music the overreaching intentionality that we direct toward each other, thereby situating music within the *Lebenswelt* at the place where we situate our fellow subjects.

Meaning and Understanding

Those two disputes, which I have summarized in outline only, return us to the concept that I suggested is central to any humane study of music—the concept of musical understanding. If music has a meaning, then it is what you understand when you understand it. The point, made emphatically in the case of language by Frege (and by Dummett on Frege's behalf),[11] ought to be apparent to an analytic

---

[10] I spell this out at length in *The Aesthetics of Music*.

[11] Sir Michael Dummett, *Frege: Philosophy of Language*, 2nd ed. (Cambridge, MA: Harvard University Press, 1981).

philosopher, though it seems to have been overlooked in much of the literature of musical aesthetics, acquiring no place either, so far as I can see, in the neuroscience of music.[12] A theory of musical meaning is a set of constraints on musical understanding—it tells us that, to understand the work, you have to grasp a certain content through hearing it or performing it, and then the question is, what is meant by "grasping a content." Clearly this is rarely if ever a matter of identifying an *object* that the music is about—not even in the case of "program music." Nor is it normally a case of hearing analogies or likenesses to common or garden states of mind.

Suppose you are listening to a homophonic piece of music—a classical raga, say, or a piece of Gregorian chant. You don't know the name or provenance of the raga, and the Latin words of the chant are unintelligible to you. Yet you listen with the greatest engagement, carried along by the music and feeling the compulsion of its heartbeat. What, in such a case, is the "content" that you grasp? You don't attribute this music to a particular subject, as though it were the voice of an identifiable person. It is a voice without a subject, so to speak: or rather, not a voice exactly, but a movement in musical space, which is not the movement of a physical thing, since no physical thing can exist in that space, but a pattern of pure intention, each step an answer to the one before. Furthermore, you don't attribute an object to the music—it is not, in your way of hearing it, unfolding a thought about some specific thing, or addressing some identifiable target. And this is as true of *La Mer* as it is of a Bach fugue. If you can attribute an object to the aboutness of music, this is, as it were, an external fact—something that you bring to the music but which is not straightforwardly contained in it.

What this suggests is that music is heard as a kind of pure aboutness —an intentional relation from which both terms, subject and object, have been deleted. You can supply the terms—say, by providing the music with a dramatic context, setting words to it, or giving it a title. But these external additions are not part of the musical content,

---

[12] See Aniruddh D. Patel, *Music, Language, and the Brain* (Oxford: Oxford University Press, 2008); Daniel J. Levitin, *This Is Your Brain on Music: Understanding a Human Obsession* (London: Atlantic Books, 2007), etc.

which must be understood, by both performer and listener, in another way. So how do we understand it?

Here are two suggestions. First, the intentional content of a piece of music belongs to it as *music*. It unfolds with the musical line, and is not some passing analogy or likeness, for the reasons already mentioned. Like a thought in language, it pervades the thing that expresses it, and takes its character from the musical syntax. If it were not so, then that in music which is most significant—namely, the development of the musical line, the way in which each moment opens the way to and is answered by the next—would be only accidentally a part of what the music means, in which case it would be hard to argue that the meaning is what must be grasped if you are to understand the music. Consider the solo violin obbligato of Bach's "Erbarme Dich mein Gott," and how this must be played in order to "capture" the meaning—the slide up onto the initial D, the imploring intonation of the top A in the second bar, the breath at the end of the bar that concludes it, the stumbling descent thereafter: all these *musical* events are propelled by the harmonic and melodic movement, through which the extramusical meaning is deepened and developed (ex. 3).

Second, our reaction to this perceived intentionality should not be seen in purely cognitive terms. It is not a matter of recognition only, but more a matter of sympathy—of "moving with" the musical line, and being moved *by* it. Here we should recall the argument that musical movement occurs in a phenomenological space, structured by a purely virtual causality, and that no sound actually moves from place to place in the musical spectrum. Yet this movement is something that we ineluctably hear. We move with the music and respond to the forces that sound in it. Again, there is an overreaching intentionality in our response to musical tones—we hear beyond them, so to speak,

Ex. 3. Bach's "Erbarme Dich mein Gott."

to the subjectivity that they reveal. Yet it is a subjectivity without a name. Unless there are words or a dramatic context to tell us *whose voice this is*, the music seems to come to us from nowhere, and from no one in particular.

Dancing with Music

Some insight can be gained into this phenomenon if we examine one of the primary responses to music, which is dancing. To dance is to *move with* something, conscious that this is what you are doing. You move with the music, and also (in old-fashioned dances) with your partner. This "moving with" is something that animals cannot do, since it involves the deliberate imitation of intentional activity located elsewhere than one's own body. That in turn demands a conception of self and other, and of the relation between them—a conception that, I have already suggested, is unavailable outside the context of first-person awareness. To say this is not to deny the very remarkable *coordination* that can exist among nonhuman animals. The ability of flocks of birds and shoals of fish to change direction suddenly, each bird or fish responding instantly to the smallest impulse from its neighbor, and the whole moving as though it were a single organism guided by a single will—this is something that inspires astonishment and wonder.

It is just here that the neuroscientists step in with talk of mirror neurons, postulating a mechanism that according to some of them (Ramachandran, for instance) is the root of self-consciousness in people.[13] That, however, is nonsense: there is no I-You intentionality that links the fish to its neighbor in the shoal, and no bird has felt that strange fascination with another's self-sufficient movement that Shakespeare conveys:

> When you do dance I wish you
> A wave of the sea, that you might ever do
> Nothing but that . . .
>   (*Winter's Tale*, 4.4)

[13] See Ramachandran, "Mirror Neurons and Imitation Learning."

Notice how Shakespeare, as ever, puts his finger on the crucial point: "when you *do* dance," and the "do" comes back in a striking enjambment into "Nothing but that." When you do dance to music, you understand the music as the source of the movement that flows through you. You are moving in sympathy with another intentional being, another source of life. Yet the thing you are dancing with is not alive, even if it is produced by someone alive. The life in the music is there *by virtue of* the fact that you can dance with it. The life in the music is the power to elicit a parallel life in you, the dancer. To put it another way: the life in the music is an *imagined* life, and the dance one way of imagining it.

This explains a fact noticed and made critical by Plato, namely, that the moral quality of a work of music rubs off on the one who dances to it. Lewd, disorderly, or aggressive music invites us to "move with" just those moral characteristics. Now, of course, we are sorely tempted beings, and our moral knowledge is often eclipsed in the moment of temptation. Whatever we learn through sympathy is likely to have only a marginal influence on our behavior. But, as Hume pointed out, our sympathies tend to coincide and reinforce each other, while our selfish desires conflict and therefore cancel each other out. Hence whatever rubs off on us through sympathy toward a work of art or the people represented in it is of immense importance. A work of music which moves through the nobility that we hear in it, as Elgar's Second Symphony does, is one that is encouraging sympathy toward that virtue, and as this sympathy accumulates, so does the work improve the moral temper of humanity, as surely Mozart did through his operas and Beethoven through his chamber works. And this is the kind of effect that Plato had in mind, when he argued against the corybantic music of his day.

You don't listen *with* a piece of music; you listen *to* it. But the "withness" of the dance is reproduced in listening. In some way you move *with* the music as you listen to it, and this movement is, or involves, a movement of sympathy. Listening is not the same as dancing: but it is more like dancing than it is like hearing. Many people hear music without listening to it. Listening involves attention—but attention to the imagined movement, and the "aboutness" that lies beyond it. The person who listens to music is being led by it in something like the way a dancer is led by the music he or she is dancing to. Listening is in some deep way like being in the presence of, and in communication with, another person, though a person known only through the selfhood that is in some way breathed through the musical line. The similarities here are not between the shape of the music and the shape of a character. They are similarities between two experiences—we hear the unattached intentionality of the musical line, and we appropriate it through sympathy, and attach it to our own experience.

Upon Nothing

In a previous stab at this topic I summarized my account of music in the following way: "Music is a movement of nothing in a space that is nowhere, with a purpose that is no-one's, in which we hear a non-existent feeling the object of which is nobody. And that is the meaning of music." (The speaker is Perictione.)[14] I would add only that it is not just the object that is a nobody: it is the subject too. Music offers us a pure aboutness that we can put to other uses, but which in its pure form has a kind of cleansing effect on the sympathetic listener: it opens us to sympathy, though with nobody in particular, readies us for the I-to-You encounter, though with nobody in particular, and speaks to us of another order of being than the one in which our embodied lives are trapped: an order of pure sympathy between subjects, without the encumbrance of an objective world. The useless space of music is, in Rilke's words, a godly home. It thereby offers an icon of the religious experience as I shall go on to describe it in the final chapter.

In the case of what was once called "absolute music," there is no way of completing the description of its "aboutness." It is about nothing in particular, or everything in general, depending how you look at it. There is no specific story about human life that is the story of Beethoven's C-sharp Minor Quartet. But in some way all human life is there. This music is not merely an intricate form that is pleasurable to listen to: it contains a soul, and that soul addresses us in the most serious of accents. There are no easy options, no fake emotions, no

[14]*Perictione in Colophon*, p. 221.

insincerities in this music, nor does it tolerate those things in you. In some way it is setting an example of the higher life, inviting you to live and feel in a purer way, to free yourself from everyday pretenses. That is why it seems to speak with such authority: it is inviting you into another and higher world, a world in which life finds its fulfillment and its goal. And my way of putting this point was to say that such music is pure aboutness—presenting neither subject nor object but the pure, ethereal intentionality, the act of intending itself, in a metaphysical space of its own. Those reductionist philosophers who think that there is no such thing as aboutness must therefore deny that music exists. Their world contains sounds, but no melodies, just as it contains brains, but no people.

Putting it that way, however, makes music seem more mysterious than it is. We know that the music is expressive, and that there is all the difference in the world between the performers who play in sympathy to its emotional atmosphere, and the performers on whom it makes no impression. To perform this music with understanding is to be at one with its "aboutness": to hear in its movement a character that you reproduce in yourself. And all those facts give the music a place at the center of our lives. Yet when we come to translate what we understand into criticism, we talk of form and structure, of key relations and harmonic progressions. We try to show how the work, despite its episodic character, is meticulously composed from phrases and sequences, how each new episode answers the last, and contributes to the ongoing musical argument. We show how the radical changes of key, already hinted at in the fugal first movement, and then emphasized in each successive episode, are foretold in the opening phrase, and how the fight between the tonalities of C-sharp and A that is ceremoniously introduced in the third bar, is maintained throughout the quartet, causing the last movement to swing round from F-sharp minor to C-sharp major only in the last few bars (ex. 4). This kind of discussion, which is the stuff of music criticism, might seem to suggest that Hanslick was right after all: that there is no such thing as "aboutness" in music, that all reference to the form of life revealed and enacted in the music is merely a metaphor, and that what we call the "life" in Beethoven's quartet is only the syntactical surprises that we come across in listening to it.

Ex. 4. Beethoven's C-sharp Minor Quartet, op. 131.

Ex. 5. Beethoven's C-sharp Minor Quartet, op. 131.

And yet we resist that conclusion. The C-sharp Minor Quartet is one of the most moving pieces that Beethoven wrote, a profound and authoritative work that speaks, as Beethoven said of his *Missa Solemnis*, "from the heart to the heart." There is, in that opening phrase, a defiant seriousness, an invitation to dialogue and sympathy, which is the real theme in all that follows. And when, in the second subject of the sixth movement, the opening phrase is echoed after many departures, you feel the strength of spirit that can remain constant through so many changes (ex. 5).

To describe this music as "profound" and "authoritative" is no flight of fancy. For such words capture the way in which we respond to it. The C-sharp Minor Quartet is inviting us to "hear it out," and to take its life into ourselves. And this is typical of the great works of instrumental music in our tradition, which demand a kind of surrender, a recognition of their authority. Even a work as abstract and architectural as *The Art of Fugue* speaks with this authority, telling you that you are not going to be the same person when you have finished with it as you were when you began.

Can we make sense of that kind of statement? The word "profound" is used in many ways, all of which are linked by chains of analogy and paronymy to the central examples of ponds, rivers, and oceans.[15] It is a profound utterance of Shakespeare's that "Full fathom five thy father lies," reminding us of the final resting place of the father in everybody's heart. It is a profound gesture of Wagner's that begins the *Ring* cycle from that bottom E-flat, the lower limit of the human voice, and which shows the transition from being to becoming, as the harmonic series spreads through the waters above. We use the word "profound" of utterances and people; of gestures and emotions; of observations and looks. Why deny the use of this term to the critic of music? Peter Kivy has made much, in recent writings, of the fact that music does not speak about things, as language does, and therefore cannot *say profound things*, in the way that works of literature can.[16] But we should not be put off by Kivy's argument. In describing a work of music as profound, we are describing its *character*, and the character of a work of music is something that we *hear in* it, and to which we respond when we respond with sympathy. You can see character in a face, a look, or a gesture. And you can hear it in a tone of voice. So too can you hear it in music.

Profundity, in music as in people, is the opposite of superficiality. A superficial theme can become the subject of a profound musical examination (Beethoven's *Diabelli Variations*), just as a profound theme can be developed in a superficial way (Mendelssohn's *Variations sérieuses*). A work may start from an impressive theme but prove itself unable to stay true to it—as does, for example, Strauss's tone poem *Also Sprach Zarathustra*, which starts from the same gesture that Schubert had used to such astonishing effect at the outset of his G Major Quartet, the unprepared change between major and minor on the tonic chord. But in Strauss the gesture is empty and bombastic—a claim

[15] Aristotle introduces the idea of "paronymous" uses through the example of "healthy," said of a person, of food, of a face, and so on. See my *Art and Imagination*, pt. 1.

[16] See *Music Alone: Philosophical Reflections on the Purely Musical Experience* (Ithaca, NY: Cornell University Press, 1993), and *A Philosophy of Music* (Oxford: Oxford University Press, 2007).

to character that the piece as a whole does not live up to. By contrast Schubert's quartet, which is one of the truly great pieces of chamber music, is consistent from start to finish, not a note denying that intense stare into the void from which the work begins.

Music, I argued, involves the creation of movement in a phenomenal space of its own; and because this movement has a temporal pulse, we can share it—as we share it when dancing.[17] Listening to music is downstream from dancing to it. It is a way of attending to a musical movement, and making it your own. As I pointed out, dancing is, in its normal manifestation, a social activity: a "dancing with." And it conveys an attitude toward self and other that is immediately translated into gestures. Sometimes you may dance alone; but then you are not really alone, since you are dancing with the music—the music becomes your partner, and you fit your movements to the music as you might fit your movements to those of a partner on the dance floor. This happens in ballet, and it reminds us of an important fact—which is that there is a great difference between the dancer who *understands* the music to which he or she is dancing, and the dancer who merely dances along with it, without understanding it. Understanding involves translating the music into gestures that are expressive in themselves, and which also lie aptly alongside the intentional content of the music.

Music and Morality

Why does it matter to us, that the music to which we are listening is profound, sincere, urgent? Why do we look in music for the moral qualities that we admire, and what hope is there of finding those qualities, in that metaphorical space where we ourselves can never venture? It is surely reasonable to suggest that we build our emotional lives through the relationships that our emotions precipitate, and that much of what we feel is the result of our various attempts to "take responsibility" for our feelings, and to shape them in accordance with the sympathetic reactions that they provoke. Emotion is, to a great

---

[17] See Scruton, *The Aesthetics of Music.*

extent, a plastic material, and it is shaped not merely by the attempt to understand its object, but also by the desire to conduct ourselves as we should in the public space by which we are surrounded. This "making outward" of the inner life is part of emotional education, and it involves learning how to bring others into fruitful relation with our feelings, so as to reap the reward of their sympathy.

Something like this can be seen in those festive, ceremonial, and ritualized occasions when people allow themselves to *enjoy* their feelings, be they feelings of joy or sorrow, and when the "joining in" experience takes over. Much of the work accomplished at these times is a work of imagination, and it is hardly surprising if the occasions when we let ourselves feel to the limit are occasions when we are moved to sympathy toward purely imagined characters. That is why the Greek tragic theater took place as part of a religious festival and a communal celebration of the city and its gods. This was the occasion in which people could rehearse their sympathetic emotions, and thereby "learn what to feel" in the difficult conditions that prevail everywhere in the human world except in the theater. (And hence there is a temptation to remake the rest of life as a theater, in which all emotions are luxuries—the temptation that we know as sentimentality.)

Those thoughts suggest that through our sympathetic responses we build our emotions, take responsibility for their outward manifestation, and that in all this there is room for a genuine *éducation sentimentale*. If the theater can play a part in this education, so too can music. When we move with the music, we are sympathizing with the life in the music. And we are opening ourselves to the "joining in" experience, moving *with* the intentional awareness contained within the musical line. We appropriate the gestures made by the music, and we "are the music while the music lasts," to borrow T. S. Eliot's well-known words. We are using the music to build our own emotional *Entäusserung*, in just the way that we might shape our sympathies in adopting the ritual gestures at a funeral or in joining a patriotic march.

If you read what music critics say about those instrumental works that they are also disposed to describe as *profound*, you will find frequent reference to musical *narrative*. The piece is described as moving *through* certain states, maybe exploring them, coming to hurdles, obstacles, and crises, and perhaps emerging from some deep gloom into the light and, by doing so, showing that *it can indeed be done*. Thus Schubert can show us stark terror in the G Major Quartet gradually interrogating itself, coming to acceptance, finding beauty and serenity in the very recognition that everything must end. Such a statement will be plausible as commentary only if the critic backs it up with a compelling description of the musical narrative. As I remarked in my earlier criticisms of Kivy, anybody can say, "here the music is sad, because of the minor key, drooping phrases, and so on." But not everybody can show how a composer like Schubert can make music that *lifts itself out of* its own despair, by purely musical devices—devices that convince us both musically and emotionally, and which show how emotional processes can be begun in music, and also concluded there. The music is taking you through something, eliciting in you sympathetic responses that might in due course be incorporated into your own inner life. You are being socialized, even by the most private and intimate of music—perhaps especially by this. (Consider those intimate gestures in Brahms's chamber music, for instance—like the slow movement of the F Minor Quintet—invitations to tenderness of a *long-term* kind, pictures of domestic love that we know can never be realized, but which remain in the soul forever, as ideals and reproaches.)

This is why critics so often praise instrumental music for its *sincerity* and criticize it for its *sentimentality*. It seems odd, at first, to describe a purely instrumental work in those terms. How can one string quartet be more sincere than another? Do violins lie? How can you say that César Franck's Piano Quintet is *sentimental*, as though it were up there, or down there, with *Bambi* and the death of Little Nell? The appositeness of those descriptions depends upon our ability to recognize "false sentiment" in gestures, movements, and dramatic sequences. A false sentiment is not just one that conceals a pretense. It is one that is wrongly directed. False sentiment is self-directed rather than other-directed. We can recognize in gestures and facial expressions the physiognomy of the self-directed person, the insincere sympathy that is counting cost and benefit, the pretense at compassion that is enjoying the suffering over which it pores. Surely, then, we can recognize this in music too? It is not absurd to hear narcissism in the slimy melodies and unctuous harmonies of late Skryabin, or an insincere sweetness in the "Agnus Dei" from Duruflé's *Requiem*. These are things that we hear not by noticing analogies but by entering into the intentionality of the musical line, hearing its aboutness, and coming to understand that it is directed not to the other but to the self.

It seems to me, therefore, that it is reasonable to attribute moral qualities to instrumental music. Nor should we balk at the suggestion that music can achieve the kind of emotional authority that we attribute to Shakespeare and Racine—that clear outlining of a moral possibility, which is also a validation of human life. The great works of music involve large-scale musical *argument*. They venture forth into difficulties and trials, which put their material to the test, so to speak, and show that melodic, harmonic, and rhythmical elements can be enhanced by trials. This is exactly what happens in Beethoven's C-sharp Minor Quartet. At the very outset you hear the augmented second of the harmonic minor scale—here B-sharp to A-natural—presented as the central gesture in a fugal subject. The interval seems to bear a huge meditative weight, like a hand held out before a judge. (See again ex. 4.) The interval returns again and again as the musical argument enfolds it, frames it, moves with it, until, in the last movement, it is serenely melodic, the same hand pressed on the heart. The profundity here is not that of a statement, but that of a state of mind, a way of reaching out to the world, which we attribute to no specific subject and connect with no specific object, but which nevertheless awakens sympathy. We hear in this gesture an open and virtuous way of relating to the world.

We single out great works of art generally, and great works of music in particular, because they *make a difference to our lives*. They grant us an intimation of the depth and worthwhileness of things. Great works of art are the remedy for our metaphysical loneliness. Even if their message is comfortless, like the ninth and tenth symphonies of Mahler, or the sixth of Tchaikovsky, it is a comforting comfortlessness, so to speak, a proof to the troubled listener that he is not alone.

If I am right, then enjoying music involves a kind of outward-going sympathetic movement. In music, as in sex and architecture, the relation between subjects can be uprooted and replaced by an arrangement of objects. And in a hundred ways the result of this is a culture of idolatry, in which freedom and personality are obliterated by intrusive images, clamoring for an addictive response. As I argued in the previous chapter, there is every reason to see this result as a "fall," and the great story told in Genesis reaches forward to incorporate these new and troubling facts. The Fall did not occur at a particular moment in time; it is a permanent feature of the human condition. We stand poised between freedom and mechanism, subject and object, end and means, beauty and ugliness, sanctity and desecration. And all those distinctions derive from the same ultimate fact, which is that we can live in openness to others, accounting for our actions and demanding an account from them, or alternatively close ourselves off from others, learn to look on them as objects, so as to retreat from the order of the covenant to the order of nature.

8

Seeking God

In this book I have been developing a conception of self-conscious subjects and their world. I have tried to show that the overreaching intentionality of interpersonal responses presents us with meanings that transcend the domain of any natural science. The "order of the covenant" emerges from the "order of nature" in something like the way the face emerges from the flesh or the movement of tones from the sequence of sounds in music. It is not an illusion or a fabrication, but a "well-founded phenomenon," to use the idiom of Leibniz. It is out there and objectively perceivable, as real as any feature of the natural world. So it is, at least, for the self-conscious subject; for all other sentient creatures, however, the order of the covenant is invisible, unknowable, and irrelevant.

The discussion has taken me into territory that is far from my starting point in the contemporary debates about religion. And it may be wondered why it is that I have lingered for so long in the realms of settling, building, and music making before returning to the theme. My intention has been to introduce the reader to two fundamental thoughts: first, that the I-You intentionality projects itself beyond the boundary of the natural world, and second, that in doing so it uncovers our religious need.

The first of those thoughts finds confirmation in music. Our musical culture, I suggested, requires us to respond to a subjectivity that lies beyond the world of objects, in a space of its own. Music *addresses* us as others address us. Of course the musical subject is purely imagined, as is the "useless space" in which it sounds. It comes before us as a nameless directedness, an objectless intentionality, the subject of which has no other reality than this. Nevertheless, music addresses us from beyond the borders of the natural world.

The second of those thoughts has been implied at several places in my argument. The order of the covenant, I suggest, cannot stand alone as a foundation of durable human communities. Societies survive when they are settled, and settlement depends upon piety and self-sacrifice. The I-You relation embraces absent generations, and others who are not clearly manifest among us. And it leads us to make sacrifices on behalf of people who cannot purchase them by a reciprocal promise. Through the "transcendent" bonds of piety we enter the realm of sacred things, of obligations that cannot be accounted for in terms of any deal that we made, and which speak of an eternal and otherworldly order. And the question then arises, whether our encounters with the sacred are in any sense veridical. To put the matter simply: is the sacred merely a human invention, or does it come to us also from God?

Art, literature, and the recorded history of mankind tell the story of our religious need, and of our quest for the being who might answer it. Whence arises that need? In the order of the covenant neighbor love grows to fill the gaps between our deals. The web of covenants binds us into it with secure threads, and surely this is comfort enough? The fact that our interpersonal intentionality strays into more metaphysical regions is of no further concern to us. Or at best, the atheist might concede, we can see it as an adaptation, a residue of old feelings of insecurity that cause us always to look out for a friend and helper, even in those circumstances where none is to be found. And seeing things in that way, we are disposed to gestures of self-sacrifice, from which we gain nothing, since the reward is recruited by our genes.

The Order of Creation

That picture, I maintain, is unacceptable. Human life is subject to constant disruption by experiences that cannot be accommodated in purely contractual terms. These experiences are not simply irrational residues, although they belong to another order of things, in which "coming to be and passing away," to use the Aristotelian idiom, are the ruling principles: the order of creation.

Physics has no use for the idea of creation. In the order of nature there is neither creation nor destruction, and what we know as objects are merely the passing shapes adopted by particles and forces on their way from the singularity at one end of the causal envelope to the singularity at the other. In the order of nature one thing morphs into its successor without any absolute loss or gain, the whole being governed by laws of conservation that forbid us to say that something is created out of nothing, or that another thing simply disappears.

In our own lives, however, we are constantly confronted with the thought of nothingness. The individuality of the "I" presents me with a strange thought: this, which I know only as subject and cannot know as object, will one day be destroyed without remainder. The self is composed of nothing and therefore leaves nothing behind. That is the dread thought contained in the wrapped figure in Böcklin's boat, who stands there like the "I" in a sentence—a sentence of death, *un arrêt de mort*.[1] The I exists on the edge of things, neither part of the physical world nor removed from it; hence it can be destroyed, leaving nothing. Just as it came into existence out of nothing, so does it escape into nothing when its hour has come.

Death, therefore, is the boundary of my world: beyond it is nothing. Sartre argued that this nothing that I anticipate at the end of life is present in all my waking moments, since it is what the self essentially is. Just as it is impossible to move my eyes so as to see the edge of my visual field, so is it impossible to shift my attention so that the subject becomes an object of its own awareness. The subject flees into nothingness before all my attempts to capture it.[2] In self-consciousness, therefore, I confront *le néant*. For us, as Sartre puts it, "nothingness lies coiled in the heart of being, like a worm."

Whatever language we choose to capture this elusive feature of our condition, we must accept that human life constantly presents us with the thought of annihilation, and of the absolute fragility of our attachments. It is as though, in the extreme situations into which we stumble, the veil of our comforts is torn suddenly asunder, and we confront another order, where being and nothingness, creation and

[1] See the troubled prose work of that title by Maurice Blanchot.
[2] Sartre, *L'Être et le néant* (Paris: Gallimard, 1943). Sartre's argument is finely explained by Sebastian Gardner, *Sartre's Being and Nothingness* (London: Continuum, 2012). On the intricate sense of death as a horizon, see J. J. Valberg, *Dream, Death, and the Self* (Princeton, NJ: Princeton University Press, 2007).

destruction, wrestle forever and with no fixed result. Gerard Manley Hopkins puts it with great force:

> O the mind, mind has mountains; cliffs of fall
> Frightful, sheer, no-man-fathomed. Hold them cheap
> May who ne'er hung there. Nor does long our small
> Durance deal with that steep or deep. Here! creep,
> Wretch, under a comfort serves in a whirlwind: all
> Life death does end and each day dies with sleep.

Secular morality remains within the order of the covenant—seeking to found obligations in contract, and to repudiate all that is imposed on the free subject from outside his will.[3] In the extreme situations, however, we see behind the order of the covenant to things that have no place in it: to those sheer cliffs, "no-man-fathomed," down one of which we shall one day fall. There is no deal that motivates the soldier who lays down his life for his country, that prompts the mother to give up everything for the sake of her crippled child, that inspires the lovers in Chikamatsu's puppet play to jump from the cliff (*Love Suicides at Sonezaki*) or Cordelia to tell the truth in answer to Lear's demand for flattery, that causes Brünnhilde to throw herself onto the funeral pyre of the faithless Siegfried, and so on through countless real instances and as many treasured works of art. The acts that stir our wonder and admiration, and the great tragic gestures put before us by art and literature, remind us that there is another world behind our daily negotiations. It is a world of absolutes, in which the ruling principles are creation and destruction, rather than agreement, obligation, and law. But certain experiences cause this world to erupt through the veil of compromise and to make itself known. Surely the power of tragedy consists not, as Aristotle argued, in arousing and purging pity and fear, but in showing that we humans can face annihilation, and yet retain our dignity as free, self-conscious beings: that we can face suffering and death as individuals, and not merely as lumps of flesh. In other words, that death can be lifted from the order of nature, and refashioned as a bearable feature of the *Lebenswelt*.

[3] Thus Hobbes, Locke, Rousseau, etc. And see again Cliteur, *The Secular Outlook*.

Death and Sacrifice

But the fear of death remains. The fear, as Larkin puts it, of

> The sure extinction that we travel to
> And shall be lost in always. Not to be here,
> Not to be anywhere,
> And soon; nothing more terrible, nothing more true.

> This is a special way of being afraid
> No trick dispels. Religion used to try,
> That vast, moth-eaten, musical brocade
> Created to pretend we never die . . .

The extinction of the subject, so that only the object remains, baffles and bewilders us. In our own case it is in a certain way unimaginable. Death is a boundary that has no other side, and it is the nothing on the other side that Larkin fears, with a fear that no trick dispels, since all tricks belong on this side of the boundary.[4]

But the death of the other is mysterious too. The overreaching intentionality that unites us to our world encounters here a closed door and beats fruitlessly against it. The dead body before me is no longer the other, but an object that belongs to him. I fear to touch it, knowing that I must treat it with reverence, since it belongs to another who has vanished. It is the proof of his nothingness and a warning that the same fate will be mine. Hence the bodies of the dead are singled out for honor. They are gifts received by those who have left them, now to be given back, relinquished by the community in a collective act of sacrifice. This relinquishing of the dead lies on the living as a duty: hence in book 11 of the *Odyssey* the spirit of Elpenor, who had fallen from the roof of Circe's palace, begs Odysseus to return to the place of his death and to give to him a ceremonial burial, lest his body lie "unwept and unburied" (ἄκλαυτον ἄθαπτον). The dead body is an object that speaks completely of nothingness: it is a sign of another

---

[4]On death as an absolute boundary, see Vladimir Jankélévitch, *La Mort* (Paris: Flammarion, 1966).

order, in which things come into being by fiat, and are swept away without cause.

Return for a moment to the discussion of sacrifice in chapter 1. The etymology of the word "sacrifice"—*sacrum facere*, to make sacred—has considerable significance, as Douglas Hedley has pointed out in his interesting book on this theme.[5] In ancient times sacrifices were conceived as ways of "making sacred," and the implication has been that it is *we* who confer sanctity on the world, through things that we do. The same implication is contained in the verb "to consecrate." Of course, we assume that the gods also participate: the consecration of a temple is also an invocation of the god who is to reside there. Nevertheless, the implication remains that it is through our own acts that the sacred comes into being. And in pagan societies the most important of those acts has been the act of sacrifice.

According to René Girard the primeval form of sacrifice is the collective murder of a victim, whose death is felt as a release from the "mimetic" conflicts of the community, and who wins sanctity by renewing the cohesion of the tribe. As I suggested in chapter 1, this theory does not in fact explain the sacred quality of the sacrificial victim, nor does it tell us what the term "sacred" really means. If sacrifices of this kind have a religious significance, I suggest, it is because they put annihilation on display. The tribe crowds into the window, to watch as the light of being is extinguished in the creature pushed into the void. What is significant is not the therapeutic effect but the spectacle, in which being and nothingness contend within the victim. That, it seems to me, is the only way in which the sacred could be suggested by such an event.

But, so conceived, the sacred is a pure abstraction—an unmediated experience of awe in the face of nothingness. It stands to be surpassed, *aufgehoben*: such would be Hegel's argument, and I agree with him. Hence I give another "myth of origins," in which I outline the two further "moments" that must be passed through, in the passage from sacrifice to sanctity: the moment of gift and the moment of forgiveness.

[5] Douglas Hedley, *Sacrifice Imagined: Violence, Atonement and the Sacred* (London: Continuum, 2010).

Giving and Forgiving

The moment of gift is illustrated by the Old Testament story of Abraham and Isaac (or Abraham and Ishmael in the Koranic version). Abraham's willingness to sacrifice his son might seem to be as sinful as the Aztec practice of mass murder on behalf of the sun god. However, Abraham was giving up something that he deeply loved, risking his own happiness and being, for a God whom he believed had the right to ask for it. In preparing to make a gift of his beloved son, he recognized that his son was in turn a gift from God.[6] He had reached a threshold, set himself and his desires aside, and was preparing to offer up what was most dear to him. He was doing this for no other reason than that God commanded it, and his failure to consult Isaac in the matter suggests a God-obsession bordering on the pathological. Both Abraham and God had passed through the boundary of the covenant that had just been struck between them—Abraham in offering, and God in commanding, the death of his son. Nothing like this was agreed (see Gen. 17). But Abraham proceeded without hesitation from the secure order of the covenant into the troubled order of creation, where rules and deals are set aside. And in doing so, he encountered a fundamental religious truth, which is that being is not an accident but a gift. This thought opens up a new moment in the unfolding of the sacred, and rituals, liturgies, sanctuaries as we now understand them are all ways of dramatizing this moment, ways of illustrating the truth that what we have and are has been given to us.[7]

The moment of forgiveness brings to the fore another religious truth, which is that sacrifice achieves reconciliation only through the sacrifice of self. This is the truth made vivid on the Cross, and subsequently embedded in all the sacred rituals of the Christian religion. Although I disagree with Girard's account of the sacred, I agree with him that the Cross marks a transition into another order of things, in which victims are no longer required. In this new order

---

[6] It is possible that Kierkegaard is working toward this position in *Fear and Trembling*; but see John Lippitt, *Kierkegaard and Fear and Trembling* (London: Routledge, 2003), for an exploration of the many-layered nature of Kierkegaard's text.

[7] For suggestive thoughts on the logic and reward of giving, see Lewis Hyde, *The Gift: Imagination and the Erotic Life of Property* (New York: Vintage Books, 1983).

it is self-sacrifice that underpins the moral life, and for the Christian the most vivid of all occurrences of the sacred is the Eucharist, which commemorates God's own supreme self-sacrifice for the sake of humankind. From this we are to learn the way of forgiveness.

The covenant demands that each person honor his obligations and receive his rights. But no one has a right to forgiveness, and no one, in the scheme of the covenant, is obliged to offer it. Forgiveness comes, when it comes, as a gift. True, it is a gift that must be earned. But it is earned by penitence, contrition, and atonement—acts that cannot be terms of a contract, but which must themselves be given if they are to rectify the fault. In this way the moment of forgiveness brings to completion the process that we observe in Abraham's half-mad sense of what he was being asked to do. It is the moment of mutual recognition, when two people lay down their resentment in an exchange of gifts.

There is a long-standing distinction in Christian theology between nature and grace. Without examining the intricate arguments that have been spun around the distinction, I refer instead to my suggestions in the last paragraph, which indicate that the things needed for the spiritual life are gifts, made present to us when we offer ourselves. The sacred comes to us when, in the midst of all our calculations, we set aside the order of the covenant and see the world, ourselves, and all that we have as given—as signs, so the Christian would put it, of God's grace.

That is why we should move on from Girard's emphasis on sacrificial violence. Much more important among sacred moments are those in which the gift idea breaks through. For example, there is the moment of falling in love. The lover experiences himself as dependent upon the other's being and bound to it. A division enters his world, between life with her and a void where she is not. In jealousy he falls into that void, and she too falls. In possession he is made anew. In all that happens between lovers, creation fights with destruction. It is not surprising, therefore, if there is a hesitation, a sense of the forbidden nature of this thing that is so much wanted. The body of the other is conceived as outside the order of the covenant, entering it from a place of inscrutable imperatives that we must obey—but obey freely.

The proximity of the sacred and the forbidden is a commonplace of anthropology. Both are invitations to transgression, and inspire equally fear and desire when we find ourselves in their presence. The point has been emphasized, in connection with erotic feelings, by Georges Bataille in a highly influential text.[8] People fall into traps that no creature bound in the order of nature could ever encounter. The experience of the sacred is the revelation, in the midst of everyday things, of another order, in which creation and destruction are the ruling principles. The great junctures of life are precisely those in which this order shines through, so that deals lose their meaning and vows come in their place. New life is a gift from the place where things are created and destroyed for no merely human reason. Birth is therefore marked by rituals of acceptance and gratitude, and by vows of protection toward the body and soul of the newborn child. Sexual love is the moment in which two people make a gift of themselves, and also prepare themselves for the sacrifices required by family and the love of children. Death is the moment when the gift of life is surrendered, and the funeral is the recognition in retrospect of this gift, and an acknowledgment that "the Lord giveth, and the Lord taketh away, blessed be the name of the Lord." As I think about these things, it seems to me to be no accident that, in all human life, the sacred, the sacramental, and the sacrificial coincide.

Our life as free beings is a life in community, and the community depends upon the order of the covenant. But communities do not endure without sacrifice. People are called upon to give their lives in times of war, to sacrifice their present comforts for the sake of their children, and to make the daily sacrifice of forgiveness, whereby they renounce vengeance and satisfaction for the sake of others in whom they have no special interest. Unless the order of creation is permitted to shine through the web of deals, the community is threatened with extinction, as the motive to sacrifice wears thin. Hence the need for rituals in which sacrifice is made present as a communal experience. Repeating these rituals is a way of uniting people around a shared need. Rites of passage are therefore instruments of social

---

[8]Georges Bataille, *L'Érotisme* (Paris: Editions de Minuit, 1957).

reproduction, and it is not surprising to discover that they are a human universal.[9]

Rituals are often embellished with an explanation. But it is a special kind of explanation: not a piece of natural science, nor a piece of abstract theology, but a myth of origins of the kind I described in chapter 5. To be sure, the myths and stories are presented in the moment of worship as items of belief. But they should be understood in another way. They are ways of tying the *Lebenswelt* to nature. This does not mean that the stories are simply pleasing fictions. They have been clung to and repeated by people in their moments of adversity. They are the surviving fragments of texts that persecuted communities have refused to relinquish in their hour of need, since they contain the answer to suffering and the vision of the order beyond disorder—the order that reveals itself, when the covenant collapses.

Cognitive Dualism and Religious Belief

Nevertheless, even if the stories are not fictions, to what reality are they pointing? The cognitive dualism that I have defended in this book implies that the world can be approached in two ways—the way of explanation, which searches for natural kinds, causal connections, and universal covering laws, and the way of understanding, which is a "calling to account," a demand for reasons and meanings. And maybe this is how we should understand the sacred and the supernatural— not as irruptions of supernatural causes into the natural order, for the idea of a "supernatural cause" is close to contradictory, but as revelations of the subject, places within the scheme of things where the question "why?" can be clearly asked, and also answered.

Any reasonable monotheism will understand God not merely as transcendental, but as related to the world in the "space of reasons," rather than in the continuum of causes. He is the answer to the question "why?" asked of the world as a whole. You may well say, with the atheists, that the question has no answer. But if you say this because

---

[9] See Arnold van Gennep, *Les rites de passage* (Paris: Emile Nourry, 1909), in which van Gennep explores the "threshold" experience (*le moment liminaire*) undergone by the participants. Rites of passage define boundaries that we cross, and in this way help us to understand the *Lebenswelt* as permanent, released from natural decay.

you think that there are no cogent "why?" questions other than those that seek for causes, then you are merely turning aside from the argument. The teleological foundation of the world is not perceivable to science, or describable in scientific terms. Hence it can be neither proved nor disproved by scientific method. It can be established only through the web of understanding, by showing, as I have tried to show in this book, that accountability lies in our nature.

I have suggested that the God of the Old Testament is inviting us into the realm of the covenant, with the promise that he too resides in it. In exploring Searle's theory of declarations and deontic powers, I translated the story of God's encounter with the patriarchs into ordinary philosophical prose. I have also suggested that there is, underlying nature and the covenant, another order of things, which reveals itself in moments of emergency, when we confront the truth that we are suspended between being and nothingness. I pointed out that the science of the human being, which sees the seat of all activity and thought in the brain, will not find, in the organism that it explores, the thing that we address in the space of reasons. The "I" is transcendental, which does not mean that it exists elsewhere, but that it exists in *another way*, as music exists in another way from sound, and God in another way from the world. The search for God often seems hopeless; but the usual grounds given for thinking this imply that the search for the other person is hopeless too. Why not say, rather, that we stand here on the edge of a mystery? In these concluding thoughts I want to approach as near as I can to that edge.

The God of the philosophers has been defined in ways that seem to set him entirely outside the sphere in which we exist and where we hope to encounter him. He is the "necessary being," the "*causa sui*," "that than which no greater can be conceived," the "final cause" of a world "ordered toward" him, and so on. All these expressions define some part of the enormous metaphysical burden that has been placed on God's shoulders by the philosophical attempts to prove his existence. I don't say that these attempts are wasted, or that they do not present us with interesting puzzles for which the postulate of God is one among the possible solutions.[10] But the God to whom

[10] No recent philosopher has been more persistent and clear in marshaling the arguments than the Calvinist Alvin Plantinga, whose thoughts have been digested in James F. Sennett,

they point is outside the envelope of causes, while our God-directed thoughts demand an encounter within that envelope, an encounter with the "real presence." God himself demands this, we believe, since he requires us to enter into a covenant with him. I cannot answer the question how it is possible that one and the same being should be outside space and time, and yet encountered as a subject within space and time. But then I cannot answer the question asked of you and me, how one and the same being can be an organism, and also a free subject who is called to account in the space of reasons. The problem of personal identity suggests that the question may have no answer. Indeed, the unanswerable nature of questions like this is part of what cognitive dualism commits us to. Many monotheistic thinkers, from Tertullian through al-Ghazālī to Kierkegaard and beyond, have suggested that faith flourishes on absurdity, since by embracing absurdity we silence the rational intellect. I say, rather, that faith asks that we learn to live with mysteries, and not to wipe them away—for in wiping them away we may wipe away the face of the world. Christians believe that they can reconcile the transcendent God with the real presence, through the doctrine of the Incarnation. But I regard that doctrine as another story, which does not explain the mystery of God's presence but merely repeats it.

Nevertheless, there is something more to be said about the relation between God and man. At several points in the argument I have touched upon Thomas Nagel's argument, that unless there are deep teleological laws governing the natural world, it is an unlikely accident that we humans are guided by our reason toward the true and the good. I incline rather to Kant's position in the *Critique of Pure Reason*, that the truth-directed nature of our understanding is transcendentally grounded. By this I mean that its validity is presupposed, even by the attempts to refute it. There is no way that a reasoning being can even entertain the idea that his thinking might be systematically false, or not amenable to correction by its own internal principles. It seems to me highly unlikely, therefore, that a case can

ed., *The Analytic Theist: An Alvin Plantinga Reader* (Grand Rapids, MI: William B. Eerdmans, 1998).

be mounted in Nagel's way, for the existence of a universe governed by final causes.

At the same time, however, subjects exist in the space of reasons, and these reasons conform to standards of validity. If it were not so, then natural law, common law, and the order of the covenant would be without foundation. If we mean by final causes the reasons, meanings, and forms of rational accountability that enable us to live as subjects in a communal world, therefore, it is provocative and unfounded to deny that final causes exist.

Here is one way of looking at the matter. The laws of physics are laws of cause and effect, which relate complex conditions to the simpler and earlier conditions from which they flow. Teleological principles can therefore leave no discernible mark in the order of nature, as physics describes it. Nevertheless, it is as though we humans orientate ourselves by such principles, rather as some animals orientate themselves by the earth's magnetic field. In the order of the covenant we are pointed in a certain *direction*, guided by reasons whose authority is intrinsic to them. If we look for the foundation of these reasons and meanings, we look always beyond the physical horizon, just as we do when we look into the eyes of another person, and ask him "why?"

To see teleological order in that way is not to accept "intelligent design." It is, I think, true that the neo-Darwinian theory, which explains the appearance of design in nature through natural selection operating on random genetic mutations, encounters serious difficulties in accounting for the basic forms and body plans of species.[11] It is now apparent that more information is required to make a viable animal than the information stored in its genetic code. But to use such facts as evidence for intelligent design is to depart from natural science. Biology seeks to explain complex phenomena like intelligence in terms of simpler phenomena like codified replication. To see intelligence as the outcome of intelligent design, by contrast, is to read the effect into the cause. It is to explain intelligence by means of intelligence, and so to make intelligence inexplicable. Sure,

---

[11] For a summary of the difficulties, see Stephen G. Meyer, *Darwin's Doubt: The Explosive Origin of Animal Life and the Case for Intelligent Design* (New York: HarperCollins, 2013).

maybe it *is* inexplicable. But that would be a theological and not a scientific claim.

The Existence of God

Our relation to God is an intentional (and hence intensional) relation, and the logicians will step in to say that you cannot quantify into an intensional context, and therefore cannot deduce from this God-directed attitude that God really exists. That is true. But in the faithful frame of mind we see creation and destruction contending for dominance, and ourselves as caught between the two. We see the world as both contingent and furnished with a reason, even if it is a reason that we cannot discover. Faith understands the world in the light of this, as a place of "coming to be and passing away." Hence there is a peculiar condition that we might call the "loss of faith," which is not simply an atheistic refusal to see nature in any terms other than those provided by the natural sciences, but a disappointed search for reasons, perhaps combined with a will to invent them. We encounter this loss of faith in the existentialism of Sartre, for whom existence is a question, and nothingness a constant presence, which is the "real presence" of the self, the *pour soi*, in all of us.

For Sartre there is no God to provide the reason for my existence; hence it is I who must provide it, and in doing so I lean on the interpersonal intentionality that points in a religious direction, but to which Sartre gives quite another and infinitely bleaker and more solitary slant. An alert reader of *Being and Nothingness*, which to my mind is a great work of post-Christian theology, will recognize that its true subject matter is the order of creation, in which annihilation and sacrifice confront us at every turn. In this work Sartre is also looking for a way of being that can be espoused completely, in the awareness that, if annihilation comes through "commitment," it comes rightly and as a gift from the void.

Sartre's *pour soi* is closely related to Kant's transcendental subject. I dissent from the more radical implications of their philosophies; but I believe that between them Kant and Sartre show us how we might use the "self" concept in order to move back toward a kind of theism.

The result will be a theism of faith, which triumphs over unbelief in something like the way described by Browning's Bishop Blougram:

> With me, faith means perpetual unbelief
> Kept quiet like the snake 'neath Michael's foot
> Who stands calm just because he feels it writhe.[12]

This unbelieving faith sees God as a subject, addressing us in this world from a realm beyond it. In Hegel's words, God is a "spiritually subjective unity," understood as such for the first time by the Jews; he is the "absolute subject," the "subjectivity that relates itself to itself."[13] He is unobservable, and knowable concretely only in the manner spelled out by Maimonides and al-Ghazālī, who tell us that we know God by the *via negativa*, through exploring the things that God is not. Few have gone so far as John Scotus Eriugena, the ninth-century Irish theologian, who wrote that "We do not know what God is. God himself does not know what He is because He is not anything. Literally God is not, for He transcends being."[14] But it is interesting to note that Scotus is saying of God just what Sartre says of the subject of consciousness. He is locating God in the realm of *le néant*.

There is no need to endorse such thoughts. The medieval work of apophatic mysticism, *The Cloud of Unknowing*, puts another gloss on God's transcendence:

> he can be well loved, but he cannot be thought. By love he can be grasped and held, but by thought, neither grasped nor held. And therefore, though it may be good at times to think specifically of the kindness and excellence of God, and though this may be a light and a part of contemplation, all the same, in the work of contemplation itself, it must be cast down and covered with a cloud of forgetting. And you must step above it stoutly but deftly, with a devout and delightful stirring of love, and struggle to pierce that darkness above you; and

---

[12] Robert Browning, "Bishop Blougram's Apology."

[13] See the Lectures of 1827, in Hegel's *Lectures on the Philosophy of Religion*, ed. Peter C. Hodgson, trans. R. F. Brown et al. (Berkeley: University of California Press, 1984–85), pp. 357, 361.

[14] John Scotus Eriugena, *Periphyseon (The Division of Nature)*, trans. I. P. Sheldon-Williams and J. J. O'Meara (Montreal: Bellarmin, 1987).

> beat on that thick cloud of unknowing with a sharp dart of longing
> love, and do not give up, whatever happens.[15]

Similar thoughts come to us from the work of mystics like Saint John of the Cross and Julian of Norwich. Such writers affirm that God is a subject, who can and must be loved. And this means that, if he exists, he is a person, marked by those features that are essential to personhood, such as self-knowledge, freedom, and the sense of right and wrong. Such a being can love us in his turn. Moreover, God, if he exists, is One, and he is Creator.

God is the end point of our search for reasons, and if there were two of him, that end point would never be reached, since there would be no being who was finally answerable. Polytheism invites its gods into the order of nature, to become "spirits" actively moving in the space where we are. They are found as you and I are found, messing around in corners of their own, often taking the form of familiar people, like the gods in Homer, in order to give worldly advice to those whom they particularly favor. To direct your prayers to such deities is to remain in the order of nature, while refusing to see it as nature.

There is a tradition of Muslim philosophy that allows only one thing to be said definitely about God, namely, that he is one, the possessor of an inimitable *tawḥīd* or oneness, which attaches to him precisely because it does not attach to him as a property that might be shared. But to insist on this point is to run the risk of contradiction. God's oneness is also a uniqueness, a way of being just the person that he is, and in spelling this out I inevitably attribute to him those properties without which he could not be a person, and could not be the object of love. Nevertheless the *tawḥīd* idea reminds us that we are attributing unity and identity to God conceived *purely as a subject*, and without reference to any facts in the order of nature, such as we might use of each other to recognize and attribute identity through time. We are raising the problem of personal identity in a form so acute that perhaps we can say nothing further in response to it. We

---

[15] *The Cloud of Unknowing and Other Works*, ed. and trans. A. C. Spearing (Harmondsworth: Penguin, 2001).

are understanding God as, so to speak, the unclothed subject, from which all marks of identity have fallen away.

We know that God, if he exists, is creator, since all this means, and all it can mean, is that he stands outside the causal envelope, as the ultimate reason for its being. It is not a metaphor to speak of God's will, any more than it is a metaphor to speak of your will when seeking to understand your actions. In neither case does this presuppose some strange metaphysical entity, the will, that acts like a sudden spark to set things in motion. For what we mean by will is the first-person accountability that I discussed in chapter 2. It is what we are looking for when, in the space of reasons, we ask the question "why?" Those who see God as bringing the world into being at a certain moment, by an act that flashes across the primordial nothingness like a thunderbolt from the hand of Zeus, fail to understand the will as it should be understood. The story of the creation, as recounted in Genesis, is one of many "myths of origins," which have meaning only because we can rewrite them in the language of reason rather than that of cause. Just as I am accountable to God for what I am and do, so is he accountable to all of us for the world in which we find ourselves. Faith means believing, as Abraham believed, that there is sufficient reason in the mind of God for all that is, and for all that is required of us, death included. Not surprisingly, therefore, faith is hard; and when the question "why?" most troubles us, we press more firmly on the snake that wriggles underfoot.

The question "why?" is addressed from I to you. It is thrust upon us in those moments in extremis when the order of creation irrupts around us. It is then that we cry out to God—who will tell us *why* we suffer, *why* we live, and *why* we die. Within the envelope of nature there are only causes. But for the eye of faith the envelope has a *telos*, a reason for its being as it is. And to have faith is to believe that the world's teleology will account for my afflictions too. In the faithful frame of mind we are aware that being is not simply a fact but also a gift, and aware that gifts have reasons. And the response of faith is to recognize that we too must give.

Readers of the Sufi and illuminist traditions in Islam will find similar thoughts to those I have adumbrated, and it seems to me that this is how we should understand the illumination (*ishrāq*) sought by Avicenna and al-Ghazālī—namely, as a place in the realm of the covenant, where sacrifice shines through. In the *Mathnawi* Rumi has the following verses:

> Someone once asked a great sheikh
> what Sufism is.
>   "The feeling of joy
> when sudden disappointment comes."

Rumi does not mean joy in the face of disappointment, but joy *because of* disappointment: the recognition that you have been asked to relinquish something, and that this too is a gift.

Faith in our time must, I believe, be founded in that way, and I welcome the kind of cognitive dualism that I have defended because it seems to me not, as Kant argued, to destroy the claims of reason in order to make room for those of faith, but rather to create the space at the edge of reason, where faith can take root and grow. But faith is not the same thing as religion. It is an attitude to the world, one that refuses to rest content with the contingency of nature. Faith looks beyond nature, asking itself what is required of *me* by way of thanks for this gift. It does not, as a rule, bother with theology; it is open to God, and actively involved in the process of making room for him, the process that Scheler called *Gottwerdung*, the becoming of God.[16]

The Nature of Religion

Many people who might call themselves agnostics or even atheists live the life of faith, or something like it—in an attitude of openness toward meanings, recognizing the sacramental moments, and giving thanks, after their fashion, for the gift of the world. Yet they adhere to no religion. So what difference does religion make?

The heart of religion is ritual, and it is a mark of religion that its rituals are meticulous. The wrong word, the wrong gesture, the wrong way of addressing the god—all such departures are not just errors but profanations. They undo the spell, by changing what was

---

[16] Max Scheler, *Vom ewigen im Menschen* (Leipzig: Der Neue Geist, 1921).

understood as a necessity into something arbitrary and improvised. The individual worshipper is allowed his own words and his own private prayers. But even when renewing his relation with God in the whispered words of thought, he needs guidance. Hence the relief offered by all religions to their devotees, in the form of set prayers, set times and places of prayer, and other such "windows onto the transcendental" where they may pause in a busy life and look out toward salvation. For Christians the Lord's Prayer, the Hail Mary, and other distillations of our relation to the divine are the talismans that comfort us, and which bear the entire authority of the religion from which they spring. Jews, Muslims, and Hindus share this experience, and Orthodox Jews carry prayers in phylacteries that attach the holy words to their bodies, as though their influence could seep through the paper into the flesh.

The liturgies of religion involve a conjuring of absent things, and an attempt to sanctify the life of the community by lifting it from the realm of nature and endowing it with a kind of reasoned necessity. They speak of ancient and unchangeable things, of things inherited from revered ancestors, of stories that transform the words and symbols of the rite into obligations. In the liturgy we are in touch with our ancestors, whom we are addressing not in the past tense, but in the eternal present, which is theirs. Hence, although rituals come into being by a kind of natural selection, and are adjusted over time, the congregation never receives them as mere inventions and certainly not as inventions of the moment. To innovate is dangerous, and departures are accepted only if they can be understood as new versions of some unchanging and eternally valid essence. Only in one other sphere do human beings adhere to this kind of absolute identity between form and content, and that is the sphere of art, in which the present moment and the eternal meaning are brought together in another way.[17]

When faith enters the realm of religion, it demands alteration and amendment for the sake of doctrine. Ordinary natural religion holds that it is what you do that counts: utter the sacred words, observe the sacred festivals, obey the law of the covenant, and you will be

---

[17] See Scruton, *Beauty: A Very Short Introduction*, chap. 8.

saved, whether or not you believe the doctrine. For faith, however, works are not enough, and maybe not even necessary. What matters is that you believe. This emphasis on faith is not a peculiarity of the Reformation. Christianity arose as a system of *belief* from behind the veil of pagan ceremony. The early Church devoted its most important efforts to solving questions of doctrine, and embodying the solution in its creed. Every Christian church has therefore centered its liturgy on a "credo," buried within the evocations and praises like the solid kernel within the fruit. In Islam faith drives ritual completely into the background, and many exhortations in the Koran begin, "O ye who believe!" Crises in both Christianity and Islam tend to be crises of doctrine rather than ritual, and when rituals grow apart, as they did between Rome and Constantinople, the separation is rewritten by the priesthood as a difference of belief.

The war between ritual and doctrine came to the fore at the Reformation. Calvin surveyed the liturgical inheritance of the Christian Church with the greatest dismay, seeing heresy and blasphemy at every turn, and demanding a complete cleansing of the Church, a reinterpretation of the Eucharist, and a removal of penitence and marriage from the list of sacraments—with dire consequences that changed the course of European history. To this day the churches are troubled by the contest between sacrificial mystery and doctrinal clarity. The first demands ancient words and solemn rites, in which the idea of sacrifice is enacted but not explained. The second demands new sermons and secular explanations, by which the vessel of the liturgy is punctured, so that the contents spill out across the floor.

The dialectical relation between ritual and doctrine, each correcting and enhancing the other, has never been more clearly exemplified than in the Jewish religion. The old religion of the Israelites arose from intense encounters with the sacred, deeply embedded in the folk memory and in oral tradition, which were steadily incorporated into a new theological vision. According to this vision the God of Israel is the one God, creator of the world, moved in all that he does by stern moral requirements, demanding obedience and granting his chosen people what he has granted to no one else, which is his law—the Torah. This law is not merely a distillation of morality. It is also a summary of those profound experiences of the sacred through

which the Israelites had sensed their apartness, and which were subsequently understood as indicating that God was indeed aware of
them, watching them, and choosing them.

Hence Orthodox Jews today—those who regard themselves as
strictly observant of *halakhah* (the path ordained by law)—are intensely attached to rituals, which govern their lives in minute particulars, concerning dress, diet, language, ceremonies, mealtimes, and
the divisions of the day. Many of these ceremonies repeat episodes
in the Bible. The seder, or Passover meal, for example, elaborately
recounts the events that surrounded the liberation of the Jews from
Egypt. Its beautiful litany asks a sequence of questions, beginning
with "why is this night different from all other nights?" And it illustrates three important features of Jewish rituals: first, that they
are (for the most part) private affairs, to be performed in the home;
second (and connectedly), that they do not involve a priest or anyone
taking the role of mediator between man and God—all Jews are directly in God's presence as the sacred words are read and the sacred
gestures performed; third, that the ceremony is one of reenactment,
as though Passover did not occur at a particular time but eternally
and constantly. There is a rabbinical saying that "in the Torah there is
no before and after"—in other words, that the events there recounted
are not to be seen as ordinary events in time, but as constantly repeated episodes in the relation of God to man. By performing the
rites of Passover, the Jew *makes himself part of the eternal story*, as he
does on all other occasions and festivals singled out as sacred. And
such is the meaning of every "myth of origins."

Likewise the Sabbath is to be treated as holy, which means as outside the ordinary flow of events. On the eve of the Sabbath man steps
out of time into the eternal, and is then at one in the stillness with
God. He is also at home with his family, and the Sabbath is simultaneously a consecration of the individual to God and a consecration
of the family as the forum in which God's law is observed. All of
Judaism is contained in the idea of the Sabbath—the day when man
looks on God's creation not as a means to satisfy this or that need
or appetite, but as an end in itself: in other words, the day when
man sees the world as God sees it, from outside and as a whole. The
Sabbath contains the essence of religion in all its higher forms: an

injunction to stop, to be futile, to repeat actions that have no explanation other than themselves, and in all this to recognize that the world is suspended between creation and destruction, and that it is up to you to renew the order of the covenant among those whom you love. At this moment faith and ritual coincide, in the shared experience of God's presence.

Death and Transcendence

Religion in its original manifestation was a remedy for death. By worshipping our ancestors, who lie buried beneath the hearth or in neighboring tombs, we refuse to acknowledge their departure. The dead are still with us, made real by our worship. Hence tombs are endowed with a permanence that is seldom matched by the homes of the living. The indestructible tomb emphasizes that death has been thwarted, and that the dead remain. Ancestors are addressed, prayed to, and in some religions even fed from the tables of their descendants. And this constant rehearsal of their presence is also a promise that we too, the living, will be immortal in our turn. This promise was renewed again as the religion of ancestor worship adapted to the monotheistic faith, and in due course wove that "vast, moth-eaten, musical brocade / Created to pretend we never die."

Should we accept Larkin's dismissive judgment? After all, we can never have evidence in the matter: no news comes to us, from the "Undiscovered country from whose bourn / No traveller returns." Why not simply put faith in survival, and assume that faith and works will save us if anything will? Mental tricks like Pascal's wager might seem to rescue the question of survival from skepticism and to drop it in the lap of faith. The problem, however, lies in the concept of survival itself. Ever since Aquinas's treatment of this topic in the *Summa Theologica* it has been evident to philosophers that the connection of the human being to his body cannot be regarded as a merely contingent matter, and that personal identity across time has to be anchored in something other than memory and aspiration. A vast literature exists on this topic, culminating in the recent remarkable book by Mark Johnston, which argues that we cannot survive death as individuals, but that in some way, through the practice of Christian *agape*, we live on in the only way that it is right to hope for.[18] As Johnston recognizes, however, this vision is nearer to Buddhism than to Christianity. His is a vision of survival without the I. And yet it is the I that projects its hopes beyond this world, and it is the overreaching intentionality of the I-to-You relation that makes it so difficult to accept that nothing awaits us save extinction.

It is at this juncture that cognitive dualism falls short. It is only self-conscious creatures that face the prospect of annihilation; yet death is an event in the order of nature. Natural science tells us that death is a dissolution, a disappearance of a small vortex of resistance to the entropy that is sweeping all things before it into the void. And because death is an event in nature, that is all we can know of it.

Or almost all. Saint Paul saw Christ's sacrifice as a redemption—a way by which Christ purchased our eternal life, through taking our sins upon himself. This idea is strange, perhaps not wholly intelligible: for how can the suffering of the innocent pay the moral debt of the guilty? Saint Paul also told us that now we see as through a glass darkly, but then face-to-face. And by "then" he meant after we had passed the threshold of death. Richard Crashaw, in a long poem inspired by Aquinas, put the thought in the following words:

> Come love! Come Lord! and that long day
> For which I languish, come away.
> When this dry soul those eyes shall see,
> And drink the unseal'd source of thee.
> When Glory's sun faith's shades shall chase,
> And for thy veil give me thy Face.

Here, it seems to me, is a way in which faith verges on hope. We can shun death as an annihilation, or greet it as a transition. We can see it as a loss of something precious, or as the gain of another way of being. It is, in a sense, up to us. When we live in full awareness and acceptance of our mortality, we see the world as making a place for us. We open ourselves to death, and accept death as our completion. Simone Weil puts the point in terms of the Christian myth of origins:

[18] Mark Johnston, *Surviving Death* (Princeton, NJ: Princeton University Press, 2011).

Man placed himself outside the current of Obedience. God chose as his punishment labour and death. Consequently labour and death, if Man undergoes them in a spirit of willingness, constitute a transference back into the current of Supreme Good which is Obedience to God.[19]

The afterlife, conceived as a condition that succeeds death in time, is an absurdity. For succession in time belongs within the causal envelope, in the space-time continuum that is the world of nature. If there is any message to be extracted from my arguments, it is that the idea of salvation—of a right relation with the creator—in no way requires eternal life, so conceived. But it *does* require an acceptance of death, and a sense that in death we are meeting our creator, the one bound to us by covenant, to whom we must account for our faults. We are returning to the place whence we emerged and hoping to be welcomed there. This is a mystical thought, and there is no way of translating it into the idiom of natural science, which speaks of before and after, not of time and eternity. Religion, as I have been considering it, does not describe the natural world but the *Lebenswelt*, the world of subjects, using allegories and myths in order to remind us at the deepest level of who and what we are. And God is the all-knowing subject who welcomes us as we pass into that other domain, beyond the veil of nature.

To approach death in such a way is therefore to draw near to God: we become, through our works of love and sacrifice, a part of the eternal order; we "pass over" into that other place, so that death is no longer a threat to us. The veil to which Crashaw refers, that hides the face of God, is the "fallen world," the world of objectified being. The life of prayer rescues us from the Fall, and prepares us for a death that we can meaningfully see as a redemption, since it unites us with the soul of the world.

---

[19] *The Need for Roots*, trans. Arthur Willis (London: Routledge, 1952), final chap.

Index of Names

■■■■■■■

Index of Subjects

■■■■■■■